The Digital Fast

Workbook

Darren Whitehead

Resource Ministry Publishing
135 5th Ave South, Suite 140
Franklin, TN 37064
www.resourceministry.com

Design by Josh Webb and Christine Birch
ISBN: 979-8-218-51535-5

Printed in the United States of America

Table of Contents

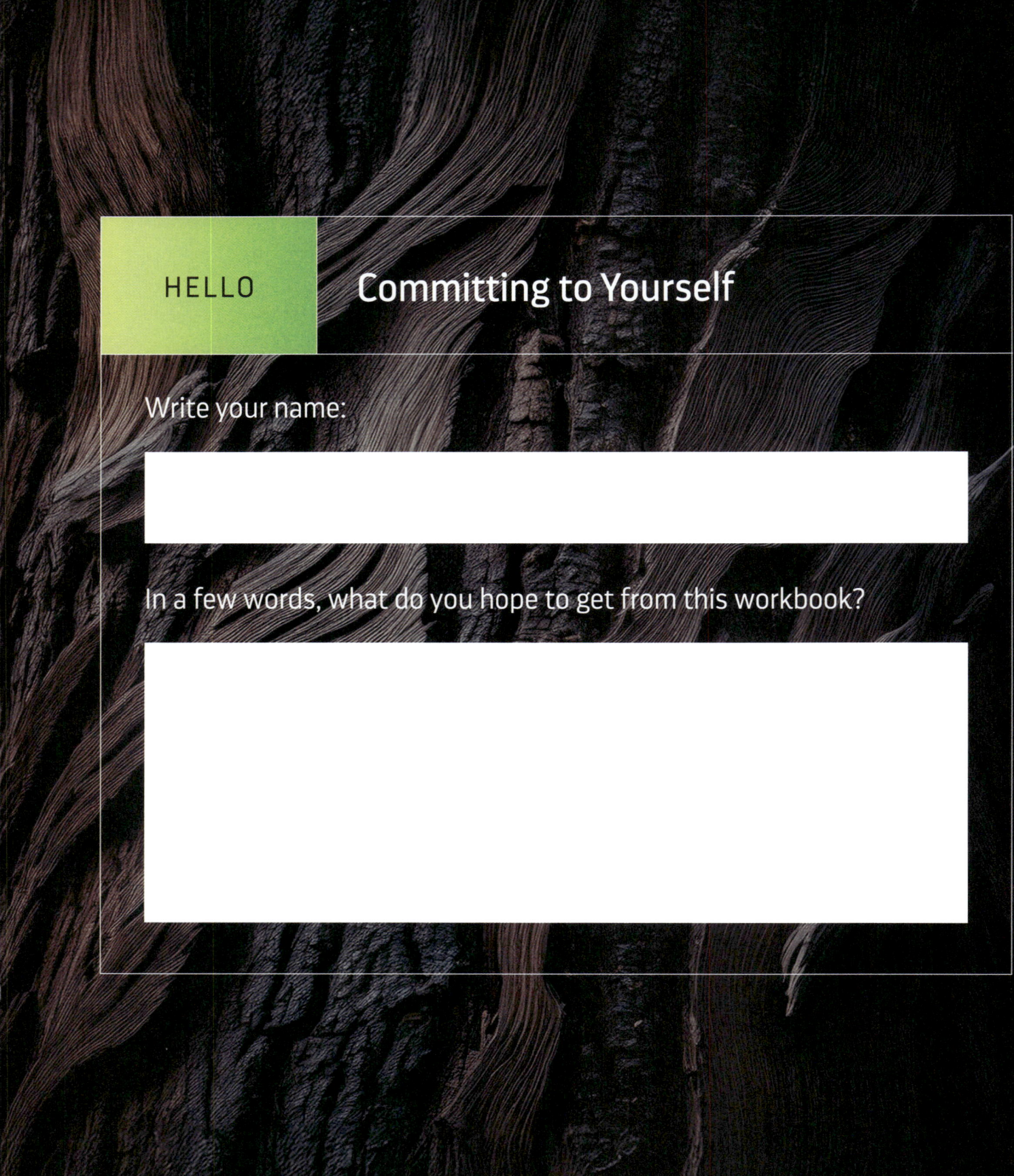

HELLO Committing to Yourself

Write your name:

In a few words, what do you hope to get from this workbook?

Welcome to The Digital Fast

We have a problem. We carry it around in our pockets all day. We interact with it first thing in the morning and in the last few moments before drifting off to fitful sleep.

Yes, I'm talking about our smartphones. And I'll be the first to admit that I love technology. I was an early adopter of the iPhone. We've been inseparable since June 29, 2007—the very first day it was released.

With my smartphone, I can manage everything from the temperature in my home to my banking, from playing music to even opening our garage door. I can do all this and more with a swipe or touch of a button. My iPhone is a camera, flashlight, GPS navigator, calendar, calculator, light switch, car key, you name it—I can control it from my phone!

But recent data (and common sense) tell us that the benefits of our devices come at a cost. Think about it: How is your relationship with digital technology and your devices? Do you feel busier than ever but somehow less productive? Do you end each day feeling mentally exhausted? Do you have trouble focusing on just one task at a time? Do you feel like your attention span is weaker than it used to be? Social scientists and anthropologists have observed that our fixation with digital devices has numbed us, sedated us, and exhausted us, leaving us feeling lonelier and more disconnected. It has lulled us to sleep and left us not fully awake to life.

As I wrestled with this problem in my own life and observed it in the life of my congregants, God eventually led us to do a church-wide digital fast. Together, we committed to abstaining from our devices so we could examine ourselves, our relationships, and our connection to God. In my years as a pastor at Church of the City, I can say the digital fast was one of the most impactful things we have ever done.

The Digital Fast is an invitation to you and your church to experience the life-changing benefits of doing a digital fast as we did. I want to share with you what we learned and give you a guide for taking your church community on a journey toward freedom and taking back your life. Over the next twenty-eight days, you will intentionally reduce digital distraction and deliberately increase spiritual devotion. By turning down the noise, you will experience the time, space, and mental clarity to listen to the voice of God.

What Is a Digital Fast?

A fast is an intentional period of time when we give something up. In this case, we're giving up our devices so we can loosen the grip they have on our attention.

You can also think about this journey as a "detox." Over the next twenty-eight days, you'll detox from the negative effects screens have on our heart, mind, body, and soul. You'll unplug from the urge to turn to your phone at the slightest hint of boredom. You'll reorient to the people and pursuits that matter.

Here is the guiding principle I want you to understand about your phone: Not all apps are created equal, and they fall into two main buckets: utility or distraction.

Utility apps are helpful tools, such as a calculator or a GPS. **Distraction** apps are designed to steal your attention, like Candy Crush or social media.

Utility apps are not ruining your life. No one is addicted to their calculator! Distraction apps, on the other hand, waste your time and drain your soul.

The goal of a digital fast is to redesign our relationship with technology, keeping the utility apps and deleting the distraction apps (for now).

By eliminating the noise, you'll reclaim your attention and redirect it to what you truly value. You'll form new habits and carry them forward after you've finished this fast—after all, the goal isn't to grit your teeth and get through the next twenty-eight days! The goal is to change. To challenge yourself. To create a new relationship with technology that will maximize its usefulness and minimize its harm for the rest of your life.

Make Your Smart Phone Dumb

Preparing for the Fast

What do I mean by "make your smartphone dumb"?

Basically, you're going to eliminate all distraction apps and only keep what's truly useful on your phone. Here's how:

1. Move anything off your phone that you can do on your computer or laptop (such as email).
2. Inventory each app and ask yourself, "Is this distracting me (or supposed to distract me) or is this something useful?"
   - Examples of distraction: social media, news apps, games, video apps, web browsers, and shopping apps
   - Examples of utility: phone, text, calendar, camera, music, weather, GPS, notes, and building/garage access
3. Delete all distraction apps for the next twenty-eight days.

Take It One Step Further

While our phones pose the biggest battle with digital distraction, I encourage you to evaluate your use of screens in general. Specifically, think about your relationship with work and entertainment. For the next twenty-eight days, I encourage you to:

- Eliminate all screens for entertainment (TV, gaming devices).
- Take work apps off your personal devices and commit to no work outside of work hours.

Overhauling your screens may feel scary—but trust the process. As challenging as it will be at times, a digital fast is a transformative experience. The benefits far outweigh the discomforts.

Benefits of a Digital Fast

People who complete a digital fast report the following benefits:

- Better sleep
- Improved posture
- Less neck and back tension
- Noticing the face and eyes of others
- Increased mental clarity
- The ability to dream for the future
- A sense of peace
- Noticing beauty in the world around you
- More awareness of the presence of God

Break the Screen Time Cycle

BY MY FRIENDS AT ARO

As part of your participation in the digital fast, you have access to an awesome product called Aro.

Aro is a screen time solution for families. It helps you spend less time on your phones and reclaim that time for the things that matter. Aro helps you develop the habit of physically putting your phone down when you want to focus, engage, connect, or simply be present.

Scan the custom *Digital Fast* QR code below to redeem your sixty-day free Aro journey or email support@goaro.com for help.

INTRO How to Use This Workbook

The Digital Fast Workbook is a companion to the book *The Digital Fast*. The book instructs you while the workbook empowers you. Learning and action are both important for transformation, so make sure you're reading the book as you make your way through the workbook.

You'll find two types of activities in this workbook:

Weekly Conversations

Daily Devotionals

Weekly Conversations

If we want to make systemic, long-lasting changes to our relationship with our devices, we must do so as a community. That's not just my opinion: Social scientists have a term called "Collective Action Problem," meaning that we are far more likely to overcome a challenge by working together. In other words, everyone agrees that addiction to devices and social media are having a detrimental impact on people's mental health and quality of life, yet no one wants to throw away their phone for fear of missing out. Our technology has become the doorway to our social interaction and connectivity to others.

This problem is too big for any one of us. But it's not too big for all of us. Together, we can discover a new way of living. Plus, it's simply more rewarding to do the digital fast together. The natural accountability keeps us on track and provides depth and richness to what we're learning.

Before starting this fast, invite others to join you—whether that's your friends, church small group, or family. Commit to gathering each week to share what you're learning. My friends at THINQ Media will be a resource for thoughtful conversation. Founded by Gabe and Rebekah Lyons, THINQ is a media and event organization that equips thought leaders to bring Christian wisdom into current culture. In keeping with each week's theme, you'll watch a compelling talk curated by THINQ from leading experts, then discuss it using the questions we'll provide.

 ## Daily Devotionals

These twenty-eight devotionals will guide you through this four-week fast. Every day, you'll read an assigned Scripture and a short teaching, then reflect on what you're learning through guided activities. These activities will get you out of the digital world and into the analog world. They're intentionally designed to engage your senses, so get ready to check boxes, draw pictures, trace your hand, and even cut up parts of this book! By the way, don't feel pressure to complete every single activity. If you miss a day, don't worry—jump back in and keep going.

INTRO	At the Trailhead

Most self-help and personal development books are highly individualistic. This is not one of those books. Regaining your life and reshaping your relationship with digital technology and your devices will not happen by simply "pulling yourself up by the bootstraps." This book is about the "very good" of God's design for relationships and communities in our lives and how we are better together. We were made for community, and we grow and flourish together, not apart (Ephesians 4:14–16).

My hope is that you will use this book as a church or community to get a God-sized vision for the kind of life God intended for all of us to enjoy together. Right now, we stand at the trailhead of our journey. As your guide, I want to give you a lay of the land of what you can expect in the chapters that follow and how, as a community, we can draw closer into Jesus's presence along the way. Why do we want to do that? Because Jesus's presence transforms the journey, and it transforms us.

"

Turn my eyes from looking at worthless things; and give me life in your ways.

Psalm 119:37 (ESV)

WEEK 1:

Detach

Becoming Human Again

by Andy Crouch

In this THINQ talk, author and speaker Andy Crouch helps us see the "magic" that technology like the smartphone has caused us to believe in and orient our lives around. He challenges us to consider how technology's instant, effortless effects are impacting our humanity and the fruit—or lack thereof—we bear in our lives.

Watch Andy's talk and create conversations around the following:

1. How does your smartphone make you feel "on"? How does it make you feel "off"?

2. Where in society do you see humans acting like machines?

3. How can you resist the "dream of alchemy" in your day-to-day life?

4. What are you doing or growing in your life now that might take eight or more years to bear fruit but, in the end, will have lasting impact like that of a 2,000-year-old olive tree?

1. my smartphone helps me feel "on" by being connected to the world, my family and my friends. It makes me feel "off" by taking me away from the little moments.

2. when online, especially if it's anonymous, people tend to forget that there's another person on the other side of that screen.

3. maybe making myself more aware of the dangers of getting "sucked" in to a life behind a screen and get out of it's chokehold.

4. I'm trying to show myself that I can do hard things. And now that Instagram is off my phone, I'm realizing more and more how much it dominated my free time.

Investigating Attention

Psalm 119:37

 Read

> *"Turn my eyes from looking at worthless things;*
> *and give me life in your ways."*
>
> Psalm 119:37 (ESV)

The design of digital technology, and particularly smartphones, is intended to be addictive and feed our propensity for distraction. It's all the more urgent, then, that we investigate the impact this technology is having on our souls. *The Digital Fast* is designed to reorient us and help us be vigilant regarding anything designed to distract us.

As you detach from your phone, you will experience physical, mental, and even emotional impacts almost immediately. Fasting of any kind is a stark contrast to most of the ways we live on a day-to-day basis. As people practicing the way of Jesus, we want to be unencumbered by the things designed to distract us from life with Jesus. So much about the way of Jesus is countercultural. We were wired by our Creator as worshippers. An opportunity always exists for the enemy of our souls to provide counterfeit gods in hopes of capturing our attention. The truth for us is that who or what we pay attention to will ultimately determine who or what we worship. So, as we begin this twenty-eight-day journey, I'm encouraging you to pay attention to what you pay attention to.

Most of the time, we do everything in our power to avoid discomfort. However, it's an essential part of fasting, and therefore, of growth. Just as our bodies feel hunger and fatigue when doing a physical fast, so our minds experience discomfort during a digital fast. What uncomfortable symptoms are you experiencing right now?

I feel a sense of loss of community and connection.

Circle the apps or websites that demand a lot of your attention.

Email	Facebook	LinkedIn	TikTok	Instagram
X	Netflix	Amazon Prime	Text	Phone
Coinbase	Robinhood	Pinterest	Spotify	YouTube
Candy Crush	Snapchat	CNN	Fox News	The New York Times
Bible App	Reddit	ChatGPT	Zoom	SHEIN

Reflect

This experience is an invitation to explore a better way. Rather than asking, "Can I detox/ fast for twenty-eight days?" instead ask, "What do I want to learn or experience in the next twenty-eight days?

> *"Attention is the beginning of devotion."*
>
> Mary Oliver

If this is true, what are you most devoted to?

I'm devoted to showing myself that I can do hard things and that I can be strong and I can find happiness outside of doom scrolling or updates on other people's lives. I want to bask in the Lord's peace rather than mankind's "peace".

✒ Respond

What do I want to learn or experience in the next twenty-eight days?

Over the next twenty-eight days, I want to . . .

LEARN

How to find peace and comfort through the Lord.

EXPERIENCE

How to cope when I don't have a social media outlet, and be able to find a substitute.

Journal a prayer asking the Spirit to reveal what you pay attention to, and make notes as he does. Ask boldly for him to transform you throughout this fast.

Lord,
Please help me to remember why I'm doing this. not for anybody but you and for myself. I need to remember that this isn't a competition, but rather a lesson.

✓≡ Activity

Swap your screen time for Scripture. Today's theme verse is Psalm 119:37 (ESV): "Turn my eyes from looking at worthless things; and give me life in your ways."

Replace the time you'd spend scrolling and instead, memorize this verse. Consider going old-school and writing it on a note card for easy access throughout your day.

Paying the Price

John 10:10

Read

Even after one day of this digital fast, you've no doubt noticed the impacts. Detachment from anything this pervasive is difficult. Maybe the pull to return to your device is stronger than you thought it would be. Maybe you just feel uncomfortable most of the time. But discomfort isn't always bad. In fact, it's refining and purifying when we're asking God to have his way with us. So, as we take this opportunity to reboot our relationship with devices, it's worth considering the price we're paying to have them in the first place. And no, I'm not talking about the monthly payments but the true cost. The cost to our relationships, our spiritual formation, and our mental health. Is it possible we're trading the infinitely valuable for the trivial?

John 10:10 tells us that the enemy comes only to steal, kill, and destroy. In this Scripture, Jesus distinctly identified the playbook of the enemy with three words. Steal. Kill. Destroy. As we reflect on our perpetual distraction, our shortened attention spans, and our need for mindless scrolling and notifications, it's worth counting what the intrusion of this technology into our lives has cost us. Our unhealthy relationship with devices is wreaking havoc on our personal, relational, and spiritual lives.

Jesus didn't just identify the playbook of the enemy in this Scripture; he also showed his own. "I have come that they may have life, and have it to the full." While the enemy's goal is to destroy a flourishing life, Jesus offers us a better way. We get to be intentional rather than controlled. We can choose digital engagement that is wise rather than being slaves to an algorithm. We can learn what truly matters to us and then prioritize those things accordingly. In these days of detachment, we have an opportunity to lean into the discomfort and rediscover what's infinitely valuable.

Reflect

The enemy pulls no punches and he is intent on our destruction. Are you aware of areas of your life where the enemy has succeeded in stealing, killing, and destroying? Are you able to believe in the flourishing life Jesus came to bring?

Look at the items below and mark the ones that have been stolen or hurt by excessive screen time.

☐ Sleep

☐ Family time

☐ Creativity

☐ Contentment

☐ Joy

☐ Peace of mind

☐ Health

☐ Ability to be present

☐ Focus

☐ Productivity

☐ Energy

☐ Social activities

☐ Hobbies

☐ Curiosity

☐ Money

☐ Time with God

🕐 Stealing Our Time

Each of us gets twenty-four hours a day—no more, no less. Assuming you're getting eight hours of sleep each night, that leave sixteen hours you're awake for activities. In the box below, each square represents one of those hours.

1. Fill in the number of squares representing the hours you look at a screen for work.

2. Get out your phone, check your average daily "screen time" before you started this fast, and fill in the corresponding blocks.

3. Fill in the number of blocks that represent how many hours you spend watching TV or playing video games each day.

4. Fill in the rest of the squares with other activities that fill your day.

HOUR 1	HOUR 2	HOUR 3	HOUR 4
HOUR 5	HOUR 6	HOUR 7	HOUR 8
HOUR 9	HOUR 10	HOUR 11	HOUR 12
HOUR 13	HOUR 14	HOUR 15	HOUR 16

🟢 Reflect

Is this how you want to spend your one, precious life? What could you fill your time with instead?

🖊 Respond

Journal a prayer asking God to give you the faith to see the life he promises.

Consider every area of your life.

Using the Wheel of Life below, fill in one or two statements that describe how you'd like your life to flourish in each area:

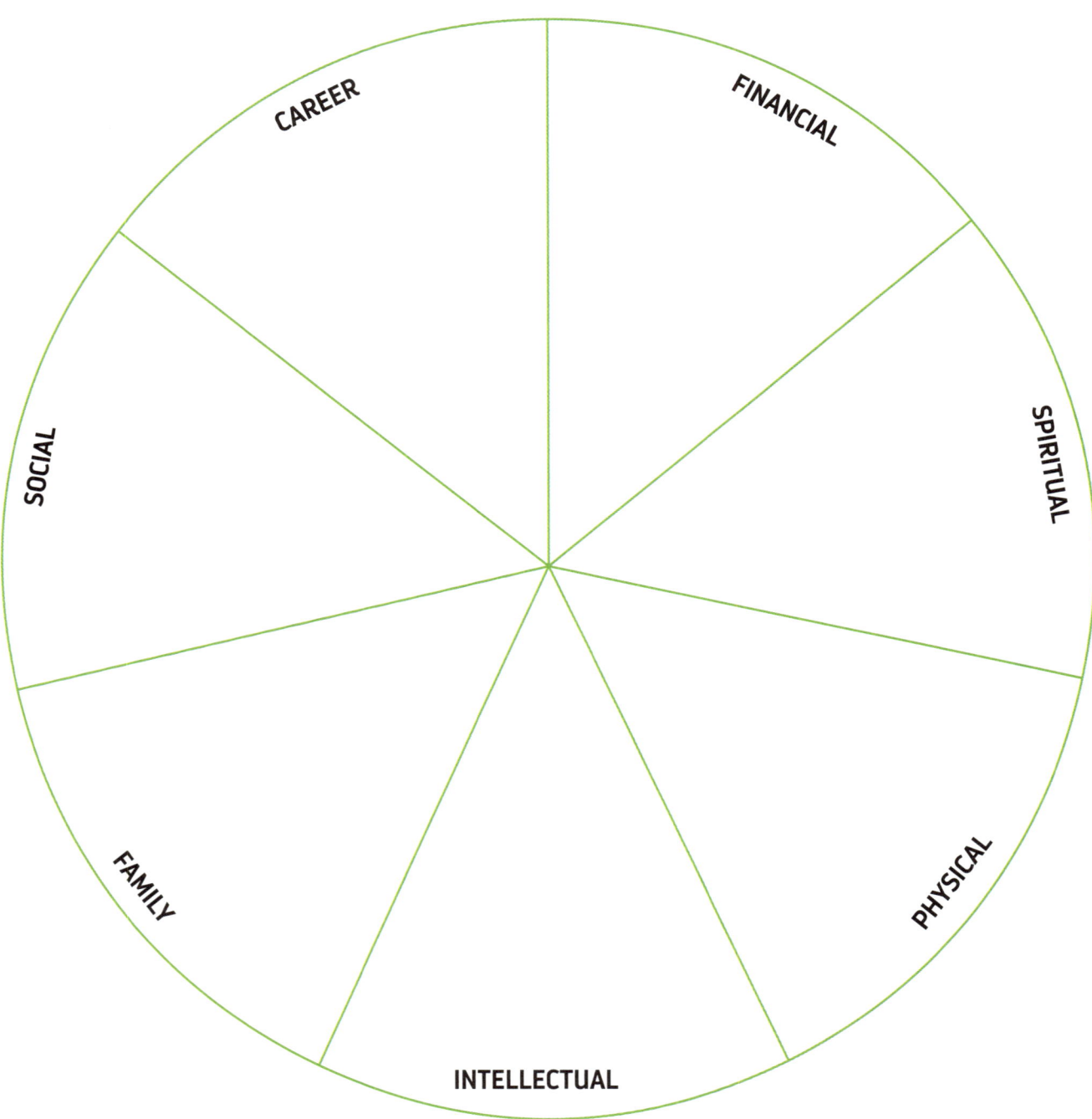

I have come that they may have life, and have it to the full.

Jesus
John 10:10 (NIV)

DAY 3

Detach to Connect

Mark 6:46–47; Luke 6:12

 ## Read

A fast is intended to be about what we are giving up, but it can also be about what we're invited into. Detaching from devices provides us the margin to assess what or who we should be connecting to instead of the glowing rectangles that have become a primary part of us. You may feel a sense of restlessness or even anxiety from not having a device in your hand. I want to encourage you to embrace that discomfort and continue to pay attention.

One of the first things I noticed when I committed to a digital fast was how present my phone had been during the first and last moments of my day. It was the first thing I looked at each morning before my feet hit the floor and the last thing I saw each night before going to sleep. I spent this precious time scrolling through the lives of others and letting emails and other messages take up real estate in my mind. This habit often robbed me of a peaceful start to the day and the rest I needed at night. But as I detached from my device, I came to regard those first and last moments of wakefulness as sacred. They provided me with the chance to direct my heart and my attention toward my heavenly Father.

Each day, before you ever pick up your phone, consider walking outside and intentionally being present in God's creation. Spend time in Scripture and connect with him before connecting to the digital world. Move your phone either out of your room at night or at least somewhere other than beside your bed. Spend those last moments of the day in prayer, trusting God to hold everything while you sleep. By reclaiming the beginning and end of each day, we are invited to remember where our provision comes from and who is sustaining it all.

Good music

Sunrises

Birdsong

Family

Nature

WHAT HAVE YOU BEEN NOTICING?

Sunsets

God's presence

The road in front of you

Smells

Sounds

People in checkout lines

> *"Finally, brothers and sisters, whatever is true, whatever is noble, whatever is right, whatever is pure, whatever is lovely, whatever is admirable—if anything is excellent or praiseworthy—think about such things."*
>
> Phillipians 4:8 (NIV)

As you detach from devices, it's time to fill your mind with other inputs. Next to each word from the verse above, list one thing you can think about instead of giving your attention to your devices.

TRUE _____   NOBLE _____

RIGHT _____   PURE _____

LOVELY _____   ADMIRABLE _____

EXCELLENT _____   PRAISEWORTHY _____

 ## Reflect

In this digital fast, we're invited into connection with God in a new way. Life can make us feel discouraged, distracted, and disconnected, but time alone with God connects us to his heart for us. We have the great privilege of a heavenly Father who is not hiding from us and who promises to reveal himself to those who seek him. How can you make it a priority today to get away and connect with the Father?

Create an invitation specifically to connect with God. Fill in the details here:

WHO

WHEN

WHERE

WHAT

WHY

Respond

Journal some best practices you'd like to adopt for the sacred times of morning and evening.

Now, distill your ideas into screen-free daily routines. Write a time stamp next to each activity. This isn't meant to be legalistic, and you can refine this as you try it out. Begin now to create new rhythms for yourself to anchor throughout this detox.

MORNING ROUTINE

----- : ----- ---

----- : ----- ---

----- : ----- ---

----- : ----- ---

----- : ----- ---

----- : ----- ---

EVENING ROUTINE

----- : ----- ---

----- : ----- ---

----- : ----- ---

----- : ----- ---

----- : ----- ---

----- : ----- ---

Consider committing to a time of extended silence and solitude this week in preparation.

It will encourage your soul.

I will commit to _____ hours of extended silence on _____ .

Seek to Find

Psalm 9:10; Psalm 14:2; Proverbs 8:17; Matthew 6:33

Read

We're connected like never before in our modern world. It takes only a few keystrokes into a search bar to know everything we've ever wanted to know about virtually anything. Gone are the days of needing physical books in front of us in order to study. While libraries, card catalogs, and stacks of encyclopedias are becoming obsolete, this digital fast gives us a rare opportunity to go analog again. There's something profound about navigating the physical pages of Scripture with all their context and richness, resisting the urge to jump to exactly the answer we need.

We're forced to dig in, read more, and seek God on the pages of his Word when we're not typing what we want and asking a search engine to do the work for us. This slowed-down pace also invites us to come to Scripture without an agenda or looking for a quick fix. Instead, we can ask God to meet us in its pages and open our eyes so that we may see wonderful things in his law (Psalm 119:18). This ancient text remains fully relevant for everything we face. We often find much more than we were originally looking for.

Hebrews 11:6 says God rewards those who earnestly seek him. And what if one of those rewards is simply a deeper knowledge of God himself? When we're seeking him, he will be found by us. We'll understand more about his heart and character, and we'll be reminded of the great redemption story he is always writing. When we're seeking him, we'll find that our hearts grow more receptive to keeping his commands, and we'll become less tolerant of sin in our lives. When we're seeking him, we'll feel our anxiety and restlessness decrease as our minds are renewed, and our hearts are at rest.

 ## Reflect

When we experience negative emotions, we often turn to our devices to cope, comfort, or numb what we're feeling. We scroll when we're bored and when we're sad, when we feel anxious and when we feel angry. Pause and think through which apps you choose when you're feeling something unpleasant.

When I'm bored, the app I usually open is _____.

When I'm sad, the app I usually open is _____.

When I'm anxious, the app I usually open is _____.

When I'm angry, the app I usually open is _____.

After spending time on these apps, I feel [circle one] better / worse.

What if our habit instead was to turn to Scripture and believe it is sufficient for all we need?

"The law of the Lord is perfect, refreshing the soul."

Psalm 19:7 (NIV)

When was the last time your soul was refreshed? How did it feel?

What do you need today? What emotions are you aware of in your own heart?

Using the Wheel of Emotions below, identify a few of the feelings rising to the surface.

Throughout this fast, return to this wheel as often as you need as you build the habit of noticing what you're feeling and bringing those emotions to the Lord.

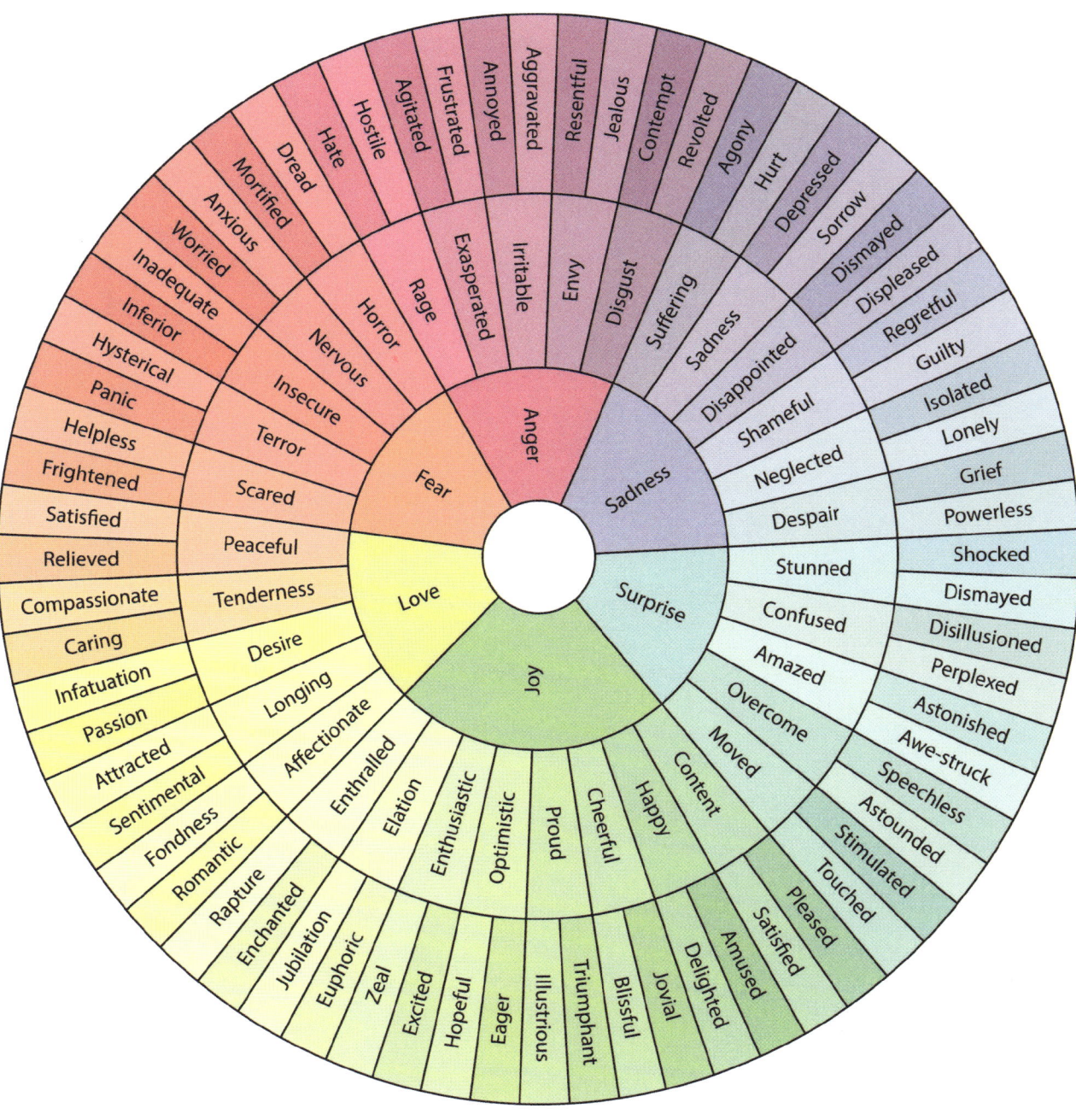

Source: "The Junto Emotion Wheel," The Junto Institute for Entrepreneurial Leadership, 2016

Respond

As part of your digital fast, consider committing to reading a physical copy of Scripture during these days. Perhaps you begin with the book of Psalms and read one per day, journaling how God meets you and what you observe about his character. Ask him to meet you in a distinct and tangible way as you seek him.

Think back: What was your very first copy of Scripture?

How old were you when you got it?

Who gave it to you?

In Chapter 5 of *The Digital Fast*, I talk about getting some analog supplies ready for your fast. Check the box if you've found or purchased these items. If you still need one or two, now's your chance!

Supplies

☐ 📖 Physical copy of Scripture

☐ ⏰ Alarm clock

☐ 🕐 Analog watch

☐ 🎲 Favorite board game(s) to play with friends and family

☐ 🎨 Supplies for a hobby you've been missing

☐ 📚 A novel that's been on your list for forever

DAY 5	# Real Rest Psalm 62:1–5; Psalm 4:8

 ## Read

You, like me, are probably old enough to remember life before the inundation of digital devices. While it can seem like digital devices have always been here, there was a time when talking to a person not in your presence meant making a phone call. If you wanted an update on someone's children or how their last vacation was, you actually had to get with them and see physical photos and hear a verbal update. Now we can know entire narratives about people without ever speaking to them. And that's just the impact of social media. But even beyond that, we have digital versions of almost everything. Digital clocks, digital calendars, digital letters called email, digital shopping, digital reading, and digital Scriptures. The constant notifications and awareness can be draining.

Does your life feel full to the brim with things to do? Do you find it hard to slow down? Does your mind race about what needs to be done today, let alone tomorrow? Has all this connectedness helped you feel truly connected? Or has it somehow led to profound disconnection? This busyness and constant activity are not what we were made for. We are people of rhythm. We need ebb and flow in order to sustain us. We need rest. We need connection with the one who created us.

During his earthly ministry, Jesus was busy. He had a full schedule but was never in a hurry. He had demands on his time, but he was not enslaved to them. And Jesus was never so busy that he didn't rest. In fact, he prioritized rest and treated it as an act of worship. One of the subtle impacts of digital technology is on our rest. Its design impacts the parts of our brain that need to shut down and be renewed. When we scroll through our phones right before sleeping, our body has to work that much harder to achieve rest. How ironic. During this fast, enjoy the gift of rest. When Jesus was tired, he rested, and you have permission to rest as well.

 ## Reflect

One of the first things that becomes apparent in a digital fast is how often our devices are used to cope with boredom or to fill space before sleep. Even though it's uncomfortable, boredom is an important step in the process of detachment so we can truly rest.

LET YOUR BRAIN BE BORED

Remember when you were in school, and you'd doodle during class? Fill the page below with random doodles. Allow your mind to wander aimlessly and experience the feeling of detachment.

Doodle Here

During this time of detachment, consider building other habits that can nourish rest. What could you start doing this week to optimize your potential for rest? Circle the activities below you'd like to try, and write a time and date next to each one:

Nap	Take a walk in nature	Breathing exercise
Get a massage	Meditate on God's Word	Journal
Take a warm bath	Do nothing (literally)	Watch the sunrise/sunset
Stretch	Play a board game	Read a novel
YOUR IDEA: _____	YOUR IDEA: _____	YOUR IDEA: _____

🖋 Respond

Do you find resting easy or difficult? Why? Reflect on your answer below:

Today's verses are Psalm 62:1–5 and Psalm 4:8. Get your Bible out and read each passage. Notice how King David describes God's character and make a list of the specific phrases and words below:

How does a knowledge of God's character free you up to rest?

Throughout this fast, be curious about how your body signals a need for rest, and then be intentional about scheduling and protecting time for it. Invite others to support and help protect that time.

Read

Sabbath is an invitation from God the Creator to us, his creation, who are wonderfully made in his image. While Sabbath is not an indictment of work—God himself worked to create all we see—it is an elevation of rest and the need for a rhythm and consistency of rest. When we accept God's invitation to Sabbath, we avoid the weariness and burnout that accompanies a life always on the go, always pushing, always striving. While the observance of Sabbath was intended for the Jewish people as part of God's law, it holds great wisdom and insight into the way God has designed us and invites us to embrace our limits.

The Sabbath is a gift God gives us every week. It's a chance to remember that we are finite, that we are not the ones keeping planets in orbit or stars in the sky. We can't mark the boundaries of the ocean, create life, or count the hairs on every head. But God can. We're not God, and the world will continue spinning if we press pause on life's demands to enjoy Sabbath rest as a gift from the Father. Sabbath invites us to a proper perspective of who God is and who we are in relation to Him. We get to remember that it doesn't all depend on us.

Along with rest, Sabbath also invites us to worship God and enjoy the gifts he's given us. It can feel indulgent or even wasteful to stop and rest, especially when we're conditioned to perpetual activity. We might feel guilty or have a sense of shame. Isn't it just like the enemy to use shame as a tactic when we realize how dependent we've become on devices, but then also use it as a tactic when we try to stop and rest? But God doesn't ever deal in shame when engaging with his children. Scripture says he delights in giving good gifts to us!

 ## Reflect

Look around your house to find old photos—the kinds you used to develop at Walgreens. Find one that fills you with delight. Maybe it was a family vacation, a graduation party, or even your wedding day. Paste the photo on the next page.

ADD PICTURE HERE

Write about this memory. What about it fills you with delight?

God loves to give us good gifts. As you reflect on this memory, make a list of the good gifts you were enjoying at the time.

Sabbath

A day of delight

Describe your current relationship to Sabbath. How do you typically spend your Sundays?

What changes would you need to make to observe a weekly day of rest?

✒ Respond

Commit to observing a Sabbath day of rest and even partnering with your family or friends to observe it together. Consider what you will and will not do to lead to rest, refreshment, and renewal.

How to Sabbath

Ironically, learning how to rest might take some work. Once we commit to practicing Sabbath, we need to figure out how to spend our time. One principle I embrace comes from Jewish theologian Abraham Joshua Heschel, who said: "If you work with your hands, Sabbath with your mind; if you work with your mind, Sabbath with your hands."

I fall into the "work with your mind" camp. So when I Sabbath, I find working with my hands quite restorative. In fact, I find yard work delightful. I love getting my hands in the dirt, tilling the soil, and creating order out of chaos.

What about you? Use the prompts below to plan your upcoming Sabbath.

I work with my . . . ☐ Hands   ☐ Mind

So I will Sabbath with my . . . ☐ Hands   ☐ Mind

Brainstorm a list of restful activities you want to try on the Sabbath:

<table>
<tr><td>DAY 7</td><td># Give or Take
John 14:27; John 16:33; Philippians 4:6–7</td></tr>
</table>

Read

When is the last time you remember experiencing total peace? When did you last feel peace about a circumstance or decision? When was the last time your heart felt buoyed by genuine peace that greater things were ahead of you? Unfortunately, digital technology and our devices often do more to take the peace out of life rather than give it. With the constant access we have to bad news, distressing information, and world events, we can be tempted toward anxiety and fear rather than peace. Thankfully, peace doesn't have to be something we only experience some of the time. Jesus has promised us peace that's not of this world.

The peace Jesus offers us cannot be contingent on the circumstances of this life and must be rooted in our expectations for the life to come. When we've run out of strength for all we face, the Holy Spirit is there to jog our memories so we remember it was never dependent on our strength to begin with. He reminds us that Jesus is our peace.

Take an inventory of your peace. Do you have the peace that only Christ can bring? The peace that holds even when all other footings slip? Has your detachment from your device revealed some anxiety or an undercurrent of worry? Jesus offers us practical peace here on earth that reaches even into the deepest parts of us, where anxieties and fears threaten and uncertainty looms. This is not the world's peace. This is not a shallow and circumstantial peace. It is a certainty that Jesus has gone to prepare a place for us and that no matter what, he's going to take us to be where he is forever. A settled confidence and expectation of what's to come can help us face and embrace what currently is. He himself is our peace.

Look up this verse and fill in the blanks:

"_____ I leave with you; my
_____ I give to you. Not as the
world gives do I give to you. Let not your
hearts be _____, neither let them
be _____."

John 14:27 (ESV)

Look up this verse and fill in the blanks:

"I have said these things to you, that in
me you may have _____. In the
world you will have _____. But take
heart; I have _____ the world."

John 16:33 (ESV)

 Reflect

What circumstances or requests do you need to present to God today rather than choosing to be anxious about them?

Philippians 4:6-7 (ESV) says,

"Do not be anxious about anything, but in everything by prayer and supplication with thanksgiving let your requests be made known to God. **And the peace of God, which surpasses all understanding, will guard your hearts and your minds in Christ Jesus.**"

On each strip to the left, write down something that's causing you anxiety. It could be a situation, a request, a conflict you're having with a person—or even the fact that you're missing your devices.

 After writing out your worries, cut them out of this book. Pray through each one, submitting them to God with petitions and thanksgiving, and physically present them to him with open hands. You can return to them over the next few days to pray over them, or you could toss them in the trash to signify that anxiety has no power over you.

Respond

Pay attention to when you experience worry or anxiety in the coming days. Make a note of the circumstances and then use an intentional practice of presenting it to God and practicing thanksgiving.

Breathe Peace in, Breathe Trouble Out

- Find a quiet place and close your eyes.

- Inhale for three seconds and exhale for six.

- After a few intentional breaths, begin to pray as you breath:

- With each inhale, accept the gift of God's peace.

- With each exhale, breath out the troubles weighing you down and surrender them to God. Think of each worry by name.

- Continue breathing and praying for 3-5 minutes.

Ask God to fulfill his promise of peace to you as you are honest about what concerns you. And take up the peace available to you and walk in it confidently.

Discover

Idol of Productivity
by Felicia Wu Song

Our digitally driven and achievement-oriented culture often turns humans into instruments, time into a hoarded resource, and productivity into a false god. Felicia Wu Song, author and professor of sociology at Westmont College, advises us to train ourselves to live in the presence of God, which fosters a mindset of abundance and freedom.

Watch Felicia's talk and create conversations around the following:

1. How have your smartphone and other digital devices made you more productive?

2. What is your view of yourself or others when you're unproductive?

3. What is God's view of productivity?

4. Felicia shares this thought by Richard Foster: "In contemporary society, our Adversary [the devil] majors in three things: noise, hurry, and crowds. If he can keep us engaged in 'much-ness' and 'manyness' he will rest satisfied." How satisfied do you think the Adversary is when he looks at your life?

5. What are some ways this week you could replace your multitasking and hypertasking with monotasking?

DAY 8

It Is Written
Matthew 4:1–11

 ## Read

When it comes to fasting, we're in good company. Today, we're going to take a look at a fast Jesus did. Before the earthly ministry of Jesus began, Scripture says he was led by the Spirit into the wilderness to be tempted by the devil. He was also fasting from food in preparation for what God had sent him to earth to do. At the end of this time, Jesus was understandably hungry, and this is when the devil approached him, offering three chances to satisfy his various appetites.

The first and most obvious appetite was his physical desire for food. Satan, knowing full well the power and authority of Jesus, offered him a quick way out of the hunger he was feeling by encouraging him to turn stones into bread. This would have been easily done for the Son of God, but he wasn't there to quickly satisfy his hunger. Secondly, Satan tempted Jesus to test God's love for him by throwing himself down from a great height. By appealing to his emotional need to feel connection with his Father during the season of fasting, Satan wanted Jesus to test God rather than trust what he knew to be true about God. The enemy's last tactic was to tempt Jesus to seize power and control. All it would require was for him to shift his allegiance away from God and worship a much lesser and inferior god.

With each temptation, Jesus utilized the same method of withstanding the devil's tactics. He brought to mind the truths of Scripture and spoke them out loud to the accuser. "It is written . . ." became the vehicle for how Jesus combated the enemy's schemes. By tempting him to satisfy his appetites, Satan was using the same ploy he used in the garden of Eden and so often uses on you and me today. *Give in now rather than waiting for something better later. Question God's love. Lean on your own understanding and take control.* The devil even turns up the dial on how great the temporal solutions would be, but those roads lead only to destruction.

 ## Reflect

During seasons of fasting, we often become aware of hidden appetites we have. By not quickly satisfying or distracting ourselves, we see attachments we didn't know were so strong. Maybe during this digital fast you're realizing how intertwined your devices have been in your emotional well-being or your desire for control. Perhaps you feel tempted to shortcut these days and satisfy those desires. But even as Satan's tactics remain the same, so does Jesus's method of combating them.

What physical appetites are you more aware of during this fast? Circle all that apply.

FOOD	ALCOHOL	SMOKING	SUGAR
SEX	SLEEP	COMFORT	ACTIVITY

What emotional appetites are you more aware of during this fast? Circle all that apply.

FRIENDSHIP	PURPOSE	CONNECTION WITH GOD
SAFETY	CONTROL	FUN & SPONTANEITY
HEALING	CLARITY	INDEPENDENCE
CELEBRATION	INTIMACY	ATTENTION
SIGNIFICANCE	BELONGING	CONFIDENCE
APPRECIATION		

Notice that our appetites alone are not problematic. In fact, they reveal how God made us. It wasn't wrong for Jesus to feel hungry after fasting forty days, but it would have been wrong to put God to the test in the way the devil suggested.

Pick a few of the appetites you selected above and reflect below. What are good and bad ways to go about getting what you want?

APPETITE	SINFUL WAYS TO SATISFY IT	GODLY WAYS TO SATISFY IT

🪶 Respond

Scriptural truth must be in us before we can effectively use it in times of temptation. As you consider what you're most tempted by during this digital fast, ask God to reveal how the words of Scripture can be used to combat the enemy's schemes. Make a written list that you can go back to and utilize as you resolve not to satisfy your temporal appetites now because you're waiting for something better later.

Temptation

Bible Verse

Write it out

Temptation

Bible Verse

Write it out

"A Bible that's falling apart usually belongs to someone who isn't."

Charles Spurgeon

It's impossible to know God's Word if we don't have a regular rhythm of studying it. Write a commitment to studying God's Word on the next page. Consider including how long you'll spend in it each day, when and where you'll read, and any tools or resources you might need to help.

My Commitment to God's Word

<table>
<tr><td>DAY 9</td><td># True Worship
Psalm 51; Proverbs 28:13; Acts 3:19</td></tr>
</table>

Read

God calls us to true worship because false worship is an ever-present danger, and our hearts are naturally drawn to worshipping false gods. In today's reading out of Psalm 51, we see David lament: "Have mercy on me, O God, according to your steadfast love; according to your abundant mercy blot out my transgressions. Wash me thoroughly from my iniquity and cleanse me from my sin! For I know my transgressions, and my sin is ever before me. Against you, you only, have I sinned and done what is evil in your sight . . . Behold, you delight in truth in the inward being, and you teach me wisdom in the secret heart" (vv. 1–6 ESV).

To engage in true worship, we must take two critical steps. The first is repentance. This is what David was practicing here. Against you have I sinned! We must turn from sin and death before we turn to God and life. Repentance is agreeing with God about our sin but also resolving to turn from it and go in the direction God is leading. Repentance isn't something we do only once; it is a regular and necessary practice because our hearts are drawn to idols and false worship. As John Calvin once wrote, "Man's nature, so to speak, is a perpetual factory of idols."

What idols has God revealed to you? What occupies your thoughts, has your allegiance, or dominates your calendar? Where does your money go? What's the last thing you think about at night and the first thing you think about in the morning? The answers to these questions often lead us to what or who we're worshipping. As people who will fight the battle with sin until we see Jesus face to face, it's important to have a regular repentance practice with the Lord. This clears the way for uninterrupted fellowship with him and ensures that no other gods take the place that's rightfully his.

🟢 Reflect

What do you stand to benefit in your relationship with God by practicing regular repentance with him?

In what ways have digital devices become an idol for you?

During this season of detachment from your devices, what can you do to ensure they remain in their rightful place while God remains in his?

Time and Money

Peter Drucker, a business management expert, once said, "Tell me what you value and I might believe you. But show me your calendar and your bank statement, and I'll show you what you really value." To help you take inventory of your "idol factory," access your **calendar** and your **bank account**. How do you spend your time and money? Make a list of the trends you see below.

HOW I SPEND MY TIME

HOW I SPEND MY MONEY

What do these patterns reveal about your values?

Do a 180

In Acts 3:19 (NIV), the apostle Peter exhorts, "Repent, then, and turn to God, so that your sins may be wiped out, that times of refreshing may come from the Lord." The act of repentance has been described as "turning around." We have a phrase for this sudden change of mind or behavior: doing a 180, referring to the geometrical measure of 180°, which takes you in the complete opposite direction.

On one side of the line, draw the idols that have captivated your heart. On the other side, write about the one true God. Ponder what it means to do a 180 and turn back to him.

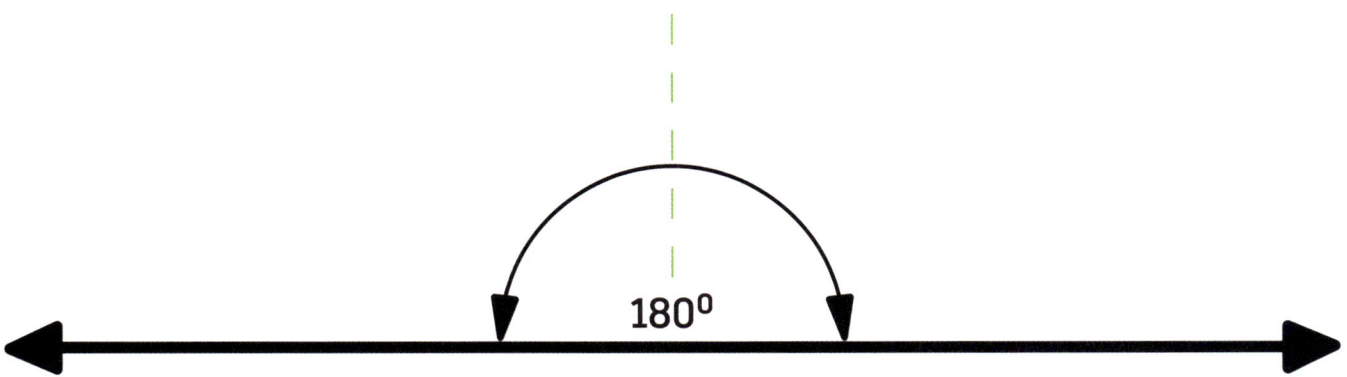

180^0

✐ Respond

Is there any relationship where you need to repent and ask someone for forgiveness? How will you practice repentance with this person? Write about any situation the Holy Spirit brings to your mind below.

Turn and Live

Ezekiel 18:21–23; 1 Thessalonians 1:9

Read

Having turned from sin and death, the next critical step to true worship is faith. It's not enough to just turn from sin or try to avoid it; we must turn to God and the life he promises us. Human effort is not enough to sustain a life free from idols. As we rely on the Spirit's power, he works for us, turning our hearts of stone to hearts of flesh and giving us the desire for the things of God. He is constantly doing a sanctifying work in us to make us more like Jesus.

In faith, we put our trust and hope in God and believe the promises he has made. We exercise faith that what he promises to give us is far superior to anything false idols promise. We embrace faith that life with him is the life we were created for and meant to live. We believe in faith that sin's temporal pleasures are outweighed by what God offers instead.

During a digital fast, one thing that becomes apparent is the instant gratification our digital devices offer us. In contrast to a life of faith, where we must trust in the goodness of God and wait for his timing, devices give us exactly what we desire right when we go looking for it. Technology has advanced in speed to the point that mere seconds are all that separate us from something we desire and the opportunity to gratify that desire. But the life of faith embraces the belief that what we can't see now, we will see later. That the waiting is worth it, and that there's satisfaction and delight to be found in walking with God.

Reflect

When was the last time you experienced satisfaction and delight in life?

What about the last time you experienced satisfaction and delight in God?

Is there something you're waiting for and trusting God to provide? What is it?

Is there any way you're tempted to satisfy that desire on your own or look elsewhere to get that need met?

Look up this verse and fill in the blanks:

"For they themselves report concerning us the kind of reception we had among you, and how you turned to God from idols to serve the _____ and _____ God."

1 Thessalonians 1:9 (ESV)

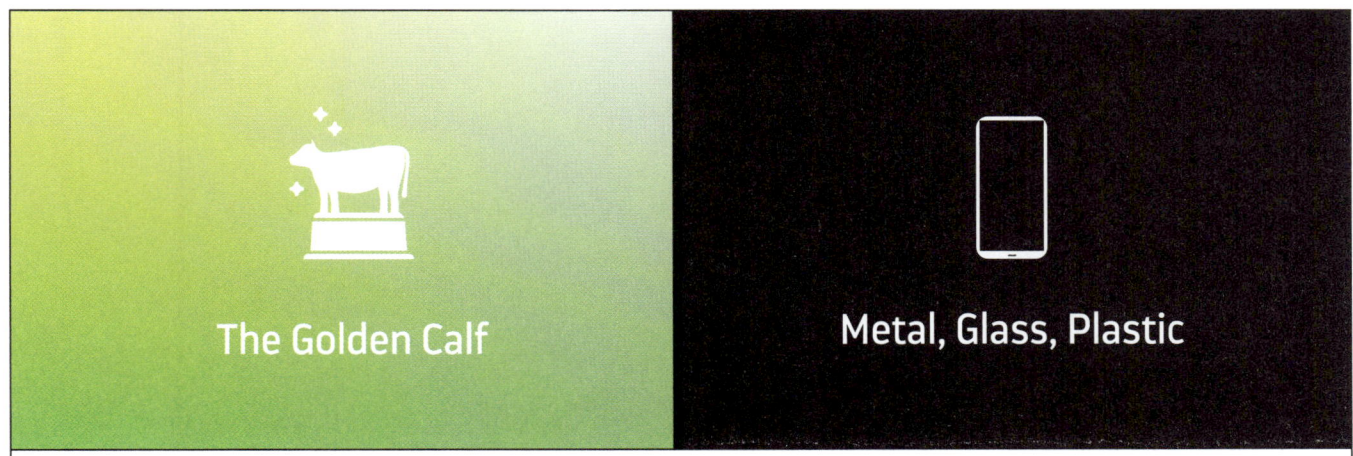

The Golden Calf

Metal, Glass, Plastic

Elohim Chay

The Living God

Elohim Chay was one of the most frequently used names for God in the Old Testament. The God of Israel was living and active among his people, unlike the idols of wood and stone the nations worshipped.

Respond

As God reveals possible idols in your life, practice reiterating your trust in him to provide what you need in his timing and his way. Embrace a posture of gratitude for his sanctifying work in your life.

TODAY, GOD, I AM TRUSTING YOU FOR:

TODAY, GOD, I GIVE THANKS TO YOU FOR:

DAY 11	# Idol Inventory
	2 Kings 22:1–23:25; Isaiah 1:16–17

 ## Read

Charles Spurgeon once said, "False gods patiently endure the existence of other false gods. Dagon can stand with Bel, and Bel with Ashtaroth; how should stone, and wood, and silver, be moved to indignation; but because God is the only living and true God, Dagon must fall before His ark; Bel must be broken, and Ashtaroth must be consumed with fire." This rather severe language serves to make a very important point. God does not tolerate false gods in our lives, and neither should we. Every idol competes for our attention and affection, drawing our hearts away from the only one worthy of our worship.

The Israelites went through a lot of trouble to melt down their jewelry and construct a golden calf to worship. However, the idols in our lives are often more subtle and even defendable. We don't think of TV shows, hobbies, sports, or our jobs as being idols. After all, there's nothing wrong with any of those things on their own. But when our hearts are being drawn to desire or even crave something other than the presence and pleasure of God, we've crossed into idol territory. Hidden idols can also be the approval of others, recognition or affirmation on social media, or achieving some measure of social status. It requires our vigilance and the Lord's kindness to reveal areas that need to be cleansed of all other gods.

An idol inventory can help us discover those hidden idols of the heart. It may sound odd, but you should almost be excited to find an idol or have the Spirit reveal one to you. Why? Because if you can identify an idol, you can remove it and replace it with true worship. This is worthy work.

🟢 Reflect

Imagine that you have identified, removed, and replaced your idols of the heart. What difference would that make in your true worship of God?

Now is the time for an idol inventory.

Consider areas in your life where an idol is promising to give you:

Protection   Relief

Power   Pleasure

Blessing   Comfort

Security   Identity

Safety   Direction

Idol Inventory

Ask the Spirit to move in your heart and draw your attention to the idols you've been worshipping. Circle the items below that receive your affection and attention more than God does:

TV shows	Family	My car
Hobbies	Power & control	Laziness
Sports	Food	My friend group
Work	Pleasure	My pets
Sex	Comfort	Exercise
Approval of others	Video games	Sleep
Recognition	Autonomy	My spouse/boy-friend/girlfriend
Affirmation	News	
Social followers	Smoking	The hope for a spouse/boyfriend/girlfriend
Status	Alcohol	
Money	Shopping	
My kids	My home	

OTHER: _____   OTHER: _____   OTHER: _____

You might feel overwhelmed or discouraged, but the point of this exercise isn't to condemn. It's to refine. Instead of trying to make changes in every area, focus on the idols that have the strongest hold over your heart.

Review the list on the previous page and identify the top three idols you're prone to worship most often. Write them below:

IDOL #1	IDOL #2	IDOL #3

As your idols are revealed, confess them to God and receive His mercy and grace to move forward in true worship. Write your prayer of confession below:

	Free Indeed
DAY 12	Romans 8:1–4; 2 Corinthians 3:17; Colossians 1:13–14

Read

The beauty of a life of true worship is that it results in true freedom. True freedom doesn't mean being unlimited in doing whatever we want. True freedom is being free to live the lives we were made for. In the same way we aren't made to be constantly connected and tethered to devices, subjected to algorithms, and fighting a consistent battle against digital distraction, we also aren't designed for unlimited freedoms and satisfying our cravings.

Being in Christ and in God's family means being free to live the life God created us to live. The Holy Spirit plays a key role in our freedom. The Spirit frees us from being enslaved to our flesh and our natural impulses and desires. He frees us to enjoy life and choose joy over anything that would take life and joy from us. The Spirit frees us to choose a countercultural way of existing that sets limits around digital technology and doesn't just drift along with the pressures of society. We were meant to live differently.

Sometimes the best way to know what freedom feels like is to realize you've been enslaved. There's no doubt been a tangible impact on your life during this fast, and much of it is probably rooted in realizing the place devices have had in your life. As today's Scripture reading reminds us, there is no condemnation for those who are in Christ Jesus because we have been forever set free from the law of sin and death and have the chance to live forward in freedom.

Reflect

Is there anywhere you feel shackled or enslaved by something in your life?

What would it look like for you to experience the Spirit's freeing power in that area?

Look up this verse and fill in the blanks:

"It is for _____ that Christ has set us _____."

Galatians 5:1 (NIV)

The Pursuit of Happiness

The U.S. Declaration of Independence named "the pursuit of happiness" an "unalienable right," meaning that it cannot be taken away from human beings. But did you know that the founding fathers used the word "happiness" differently than we do today?

They derived "happiness" from the Greek word *eudaimonia*, which was the action of pursuing virtue resulting in the well-being and flourishing of people. Happiness is not about self-indulgence or acquiring things. It's not about likes and comments and shares. It's about the freedom to choose what is good and right.

With that context, reflect below on your digital life. How does your time spent scrolling, browsing, watching, and consuming impact your pursuit of happiness?

What limits could you set on your devices to ensure that you're pursuing what is right and virtuous?

Respond

Write your own "Declaration of Independence" from digital distraction and declare what kind of life and freedom you want to enjoy.

Declaration of Independence

Signed _____ Date _____

<table>
<tr><td>DAY 13</td><td>

Guided Gaze

John 14:16–17, 25–26; John 16:13–14
</td></tr>
</table>

Read

Here on Day 13, it's comforting to remember that we're not left alone on this journey. We don't have to muster up our best behavior or grit our teeth for the remainer of our fast. We have the Holy Spirit of God with us, and that means we have access to the same power that raised Christ from the dead. One of the Spirit's main roles is to remind believers who Jesus is and what he has done for us. In short, he specializes in guiding our gaze back to Jesus time and time again.

We need our gaze guided back to Jesus because we need to remind ourselves daily of the gospel story and its power. In a digitally saturated world, the beauty of the gospel is far too easy for us to forget. The Spirit is our Helper, who continually shows us the lengths God went to in order to rescue us and bring us into his family and give us new life through his Son. When we consider the lengths God went to for us, it makes any discomfort we experience on this fast pale in comparison.

The truth of the gospel is that we were hopeless, separated from God, and in need of a way to be reconciled to him. He did the unimaginable in sending his Son to the earth to be the personification of perfect obedience and sacrifice. Through the shedding of his perfect blood, he made a way back to God for everyone who believes. Now, through the gift of the Holy Spirit, we can experience the peace that comes from knowing that the difficulties of this life are fleeting and that a place of joy and rest is being prepared for us.

Reflect

What could you do this week to focus your gaze more on Jesus and his gospel? What difference would that make?

 # Respond

From the list below, circle three characteristics of God you've experienced recently. Reflect on how you've seen him show up in those ways. Spend time with God, offering him praise, thanks, and gratitude for who he is and what he has done in your life.

God is . . .

GRACIOUS

MERCIFUL

SLOW TO ANGER

PATIENT

GENEROUS

JUST

FORGIVING

IN CONTROL

ALL-KNOWING

LOVING

PRESENT
EVERYWHERE

INFINITE

ALL-POWERFUL

UNCHANGING

HOLY

COMPASSIONATE

CREATIVE

FAITHFUL

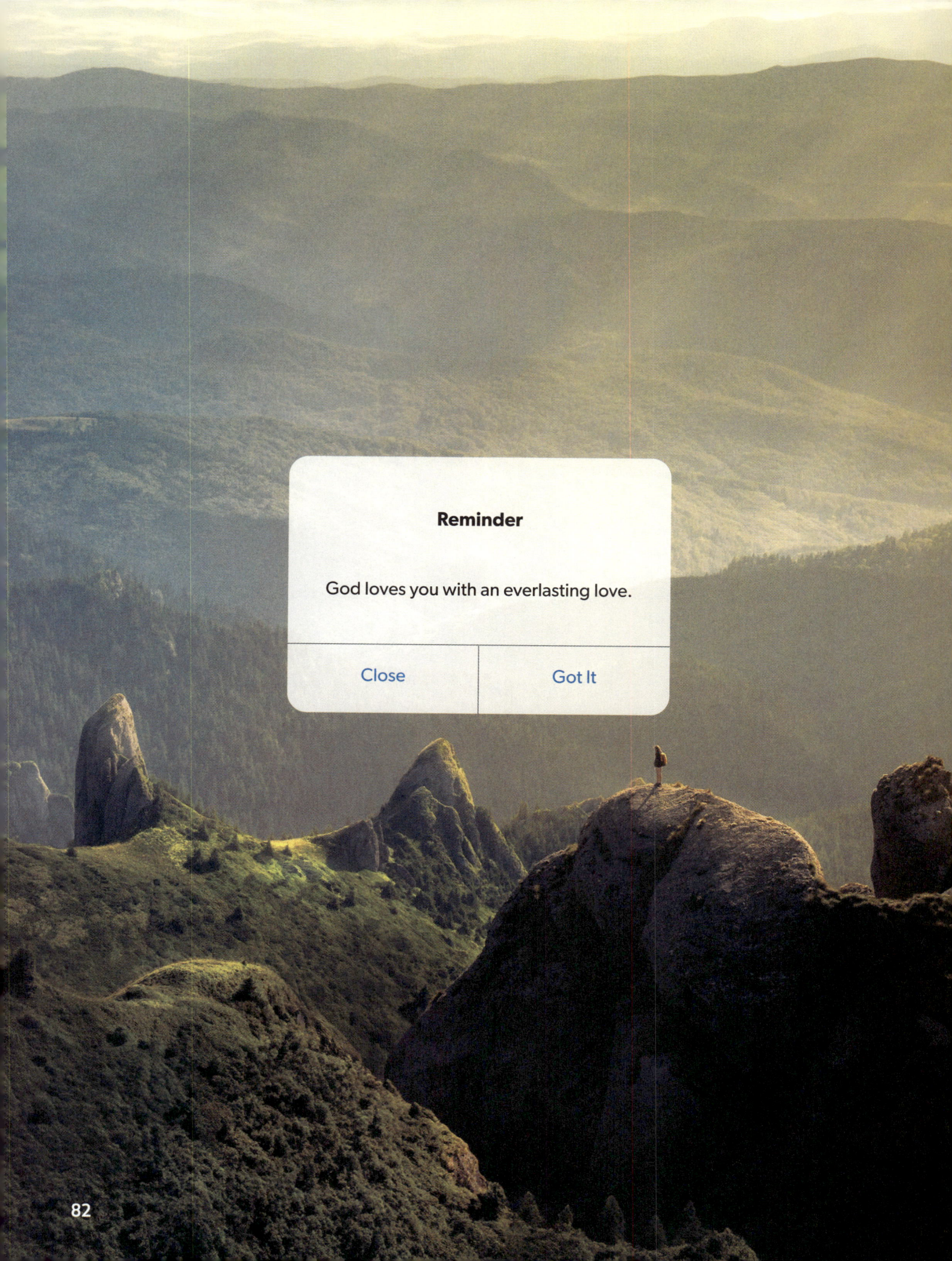

Reminder

God loves you with an everlasting love.

| Close | Got It |

📣 Good News

The word "gospel" is derived from the Greek word *euangelion*, which translates to "good news." It's the story of the life, death, and resurrection of Jesus—and how his sacrifice reconciles us to God and heals the brokenness in all creation.

Write down three words that capture how you feel in response to the gospel.

By contrast, our devices are usually a source of bad news. A tragedy occurs halfway around the world, and minutes later, it shows up as a notification on our screens. When we doomscroll, we end up feeling sad, anxious, and angry about the state of the world. We pick up burdens that were never ours to carry.

Which do you consume more: the good news of the gospel or bad news from the world?

When we guide our gaze back to Jesus, we're reminded that Jesus took the sin of the world upon his shoulders. And one day, "He will wipe away every tear from their eyes, and death shall be no more, neither shall there be mourning, nor crying, nor pain anymore, for the former things have passed away" (Revelation 21:4 ESV).

How does remembering the good news of Jesus change your relationship to the "here and now" news?

<table>
<tr><td>

DAY 14

</td><td>

Thanks

Psalm 95:1–7; Psalm 136:26; Colossians 3:17; 1 Thessalonians 5:18

</td></tr>
</table>

 ## Read

Thankfulness is a secret weapon. We express gratitude in worship because God has given us so many reasons to be thankful. Praise and thanks go hand-in-hand in our worship as we reflect back to God the many ways he has demonstrated his goodness and faithfulness to us. We often thank him for what he's done and the good things that have happened, but have you ever thought of thanking him for what hasn't happened?

"For the Lord God is a sun and shield; the Lord bestows favor and honor. No good thing does he withhold from those who walk uprightly" (Psalm 84:11 ESV). I think most of us can thank God for being our sun. He lights our way. He shines the light of his love on us. He is the light of the world. But when was the last time you thanked God for being your shield? He shields you without even breaking a sweat. How much danger and risk has God shielded you from over the whole of your life? It's incalculable!

Every time your car hasn't broken down. Every illness not resulting in further harm or death. Every night of protection inside your home. Every time you've arrived to a destination by plane or car without incident or accident. Every storm. Every trial. Every difficulty. The Lord is always shielding us in a million ways we're unaware of. We're still here. We still know he's good. He's promised to go before and to hem us in. He's promised to be our rear guard and to light our way. He's promised us a future and hope, not harm. He does what is for our good and brings him the most glory.

 ## Reflect

How could you incorporate more time to thank God for who he is and what he has done in your life? How could that change your perspective on your circumstances and relationships?

A Sun and a Shield

Reflect on the past few years of your life. How has God been your sun—your source of warmth, comfort, guidance, and life? How has he been your shield—your source of protection and safety?

Capture your memories on the corresponding side below.

 ## Respond

Consider establishing a daily gratitude practice where you ask God to remind you of both what he's provided for you and what he's preserved you from. Write down these points of gratitude as an exercise in thankfulness, starting today:

TODAY, I AM THANKFUL FOR

Ideas for giving thanks every day

◯   Write thank-you notes.

◯   Keep a gratitude journal.

◯   Over dinner, have everyone share five things you're thankful for from the day.

◯   Commit to exchanging texts with your spouse or a friend, telling each other what you're grateful for.

◯   Buy a whiteboard and write a fresh gratitude list on it every morning.

🎞️ Your Praise Mixtape

Long before we all carried the world's musical catalog in our pockets, we had these things called "mixtapes," where we'd curate our own playlists and record them on cassette tapes. Those were the days.

Music is a powerful tool for praise and thanksgiving. Slow down and ponder the songs that consistently fill your heart with gratitude for who God is and what he has done. Make a personal playlist below, then carve out time to actually sit, savor the music, and praise God.

FAVORITE LYRICS

Halfway Point Check-In

You're halfway through the digital fast! Take a moment to assess how you're doing.

Using the scales below, rate how you're doing in each area:

Mental Alertness

Very Poor   1   2   3   4   5   6   7   8   9   10   Exceptional

Creativity

Very Poor   1   2   3   4   5   6   7   8   9   10   Exceptional

Quality of Sleep

Very Poor   1   2   3   4   5   6   7   8   9   10   Exceptional

Sense of Peace

Very Poor   1   2   3   4   5   6   7   8   9   10   Exceptional

Quality Time with Friends and Family

Very Poor   1   2   3   4   5   6   7   8   9   10   Exceptional

Connection with God

Very Poor   1   2   3   4   5   6   7   8   9   10   Exceptional

On Day 2, "Paying the Price," you did a time audit of how many waking hours you spent on devices before this fast. Go back and observe what you put down.

Using the boxes below, do another audit showing how your habits have shifted. How do you spend your waking hours now? Label each box.

HOUR 1	HOUR 2	HOUR 3	HOUR 4
HOUR 5	HOUR 6	HOUR 7	HOUR 8
HOUR 9	HOUR 10	HOUR 11	HOUR 12
HOUR 13	HOUR 14	HOUR 15	HOUR 16

Delight

THINQ

Weekly Conversation 3

Numb Generations
by Dr. Kara Powell

Dr. Kara Powell, executive director of the Fuller Youth Institute and chief of leadership formation at Fuller Theological Seminary, calls out how kids and parents are so distracted and numbed by technology that they miss important moments together. She challenges us to be more attentive and available, to create and relish time with one another and with God.

Watch Kara's talk and create conversations around the following:

1. In what ways have you experienced the numbing effects of smartphones and other technology?

2. In contrast, describe a time when you experienced joy or delight when you intentionally turned screens off and were fully present in the moment.

3. How do you envision the video at the end of your life depicting your fully present moments?

4. What habits can your change to have the "best, longest, and most exhilarating" video of all?

Refreshing the Soul

Psalm 19:7–11

Read

We're over the halfway mark of our fast, and today we read that the law of the Lord is perfect. The law of the Lord, as referenced in Psalm 19:7, is Scripture, God's revelation of himself to us on the pages of our Bibles. Scripture is perfect because its author is. Since God's Word embodies perfection, you and I don't have to expend any effort attempting it. However, the promise goes a step further than perfection. Not only is God's Word perfect, it's guaranteed to refresh the soul when we delight in it. Isn't that what this digital fast is all about? We are experiencing a soul refresh.

In studying the meaning of the word refreshing, we find a desirable list. Take some deep breaths and read the list of synonyms on the next page slowly. Perhaps you slow down long enough to utter "thank you" to Jesus between each one. Breathe in his promise, then breathe out your thankfulness to him.

This is the promise God makes to you—refreshment for your soul.

Only God, through his Word, can both invigorate and quiet us. Only he can revive us and then turn around and give us rest. He knows everything we need, and he has promised to provide it in exactly the right season in exactly the right way. To lay hold of this refreshment for our souls, we must be taking in the words of Scripture. Hebrews 4:12 tells us the Word of God is alive and active, but it can't be active for us if it's not first active in us. Today, pray the promise of God back to Him. Ask Him to refresh your soul as you read his Word.

Reflect

When was the last time your soul felt refreshed?

Refresh

To take a breath

To have room and margin

To find relief

To find support

To revive

To rest

To quiet

What particular circumstances help you feel refreshed?

Have you experienced the refreshment that comes from Scripture? If so, describe what it's like. And if not, what is keeping you from being refreshed by Scripture?

Look up this verse and fill in the blanks:

"The law of the Lord is _____,
reviving the soul;
the testimony of the Lord is _____,
making wise the simple;
the precepts of the Lord are _____,
rejoicing the heart;
the commandment of the Lord is _____,
enlightening the eyes;
the fear of the Lord is _____,
enduring forever;
the rules of the Lord are _____,
and righteous altogether."

Psalm 19:7–9 (ESV)

Respond

For this second half of our digital fast, we have an opportunity to begin determining what life will look like post-fast. Consider the practices that refresh you and begin thinking about how they can remain part of your regular rhythm.

ACTIVITIES THAT REFRESH ME

DAY 16

Everything Good and Perfect

Matthew 7:11; James 1:17

 ## Read

Are you someone who likes to give great gifts? Do you delight in finding the perfect thing for that special someone because you know they'll love it? Scripture says that your Father in heaven, the Father of heavenly lights, has long delighted in giving good gifts. Every good gift is from him, and because it's from him, it's perfect. All the good in your life can be traced back to God. He's its author.

My guess is, if you sat down with a blank piece of paper and began listing the good things in your life, you would fill page after page with things big and small, people far and near, and opportunities past and present. I bet there are even things on that list that were initially bad or painful that you've now come to regard as good because of their impact on your life for the better. And even when we lose sight of God as the greatest gift giver, he does not change like shifting shadows. He doesn't need to pivot or think on his feet or adjust course. He's God. We can trust him for the good and perfect gifts in our future because of his abundant faithfulness in our past. In last week. In yesterday. Even in waking up today.

In the same way a parent wants to give good gifts to their child, we have the promise that God, as a loving Father, feels the same way toward us! We don't have to be tempted to hedge our bets and make fail-safe plans to come through on our own in case he doesn't. We can simply trust that his plans for us are good and perfect because he's never been anything but faithful.

Every good gift and every perfect gift is from above, coming down from the Father of lights, with whom there is no variation or shadow due to change.

James 1:17 (ESV)

 **Reflect**

As you reflect on God's faithfulness and his good gifts, is there anything you're praying for and need the faith to trust God's character?

How can you remind yourself that he doesn't withhold good from his children?

 **Respond**

Consider writing down that list of good gifts. Each morning, choose one and journal a prayer of thanksgiving to God. Ask him to help you look at his past faithfulness as an assurance of his future faithfulness.

The Shopping List

When was the last time you surprised your spouse, kids, or best friend with a gift? Today could be the next occasion. Have fun brainstorming a shopping list for your loved ones. Then, pick an item or two to buy and deliver. The gift doesn't have to be expensive. You could even do something free around the house, like write a note or make dinner.

Name	Name	Name
Gift Idea	Gift Idea	Gift Idea

Name	Name	Name
Gift Idea	Gift Idea	Gift Idea

Sticky Note Prayers

1. Find a stack of sticky notes.

2. On each one, write either a good gift you're grateful for, or a good gift you're asking God for.

3. Put each item in its appropriate column, praying over them and giving thanks as you go.

4. Over the coming days, pay attention to how God answers your prayers, and move the "please" items to the "thank you" column.

Please	Thank You

DAY 17

Designed for Delight

Genesis 1:26–27; Psalm 139:13–16

 Read

As we consider the concept of delight, I wonder if you've ever thought about the fact that even your capacity to delight was designed by God. There are specific aspects of God's creation work that he knew would delight you. As you've detached from devices, have you felt your capacity for delight grow? When we're no longer sedated, things take on more color and vibrance, and we begin to notice what had been fading into the background due to the glow of our phones.

If you've ever held a newborn baby, you know. Our God is creative. If you've ever marveled at the many ways the human body works, you know. God's design is second to none. What's even more amazing is that God had us in mind before he created this world. Long ago, he knew your purpose in life, and he designed you for delight. He formed you specifically to live in your time and place. He created good works for you in advance. Then, he created a whole world for you to delight in.

As we move closer to the conclusion of this digital fast, it will be important to begin thinking about how you want your life to look. As God created such beauty and artistry, you have the chance to design a life of intentionality and delight. You can protect yourself from becoming sedated again by devices, and you can prioritize the wonders of God's creation. By being specific and determining how you'll engage rather than letting devices decide for you, you can craft a life that embraces the delight you were created for.

🌿 Reflect

Focus on one aspect of how God has uniquely created you. You are one of the delights he has made! Do you struggle to see yourself this way?

How could you comprehend his great love for you today?

🖋 Respond

What has delighted you during these digitally free days? How have you seen your capacity for delight grow?

What delights would you like to focus on during the remainder of the fast?

Make a bucket list of delights you'd like to enjoy at some point during the rest of the fast.

My Bucket List of Delights

Daily Delight

Plan to do something every day this upcoming week that fills you with delight. Double the fun by inviting someone to join you.

MONDAY	TUESDAY	WEDNESDAY	THURSDAY

FRIDAY	SATURDAY	SUNDAY

Give God
a Hand

Trace your hand on this page.

Inside the shape of your hand, write down at least ten traits that make you unique—your personality, your looks, your skills. Reflect on how God designed you and meditate on the fact that he delights in you as his beloved creation.

A Celebration of Solitude

Matthew 6:6; Luke 5:15–16; Luke 6:12

Read

The practice of solitude involves scheduling alone time with just you and God. While a daily rhythm of solitude with God such as a devotional time is certainly beneficial, the practice of lengthier time alone with him provides a gift not found as often in a shorter daily practice. In rhythms of solitude, we abstain from other distractions or interruptions that could interfere with our experience of being alone with God.

Jesus regularly practiced solitude and prioritized time alone with God both before and after engaging in ministry. He guarded the time with His father zealously and organized His life around it. Jesus knew he needed that time to connect and be alone with the Father. In an age saturated by distraction, alone time can feel uncomfortable, and the silence may be deafening. Without phones or other devices to fill the void, being alone can be unsettling or even cause anxiety. But especially when we're already engaging in a practice of fasting, solitude provides us communion with God unhampered by the competition of social media, relational pressures, or other mental and emotional stimulation.

In practicing solitude, we have the opportunity to hear from the Lord and address issues he brings to our attention without the distractions of our normal lives. Pushing through the discomfort of aloneness will help us tune out the noise and focus intently on the leadership of the Spirit. There can be great delight in a regular practice of solitude, and it can ensure a necessary respite from the influx of less important things that fight for our time.

🟢 Reflect

Does the idea of solitude make you feel anxious or uncomfortable? If so, what drives those feelings?

What are some reasons you might resist the idea of solitude?

Look up today's Scriptures: Matthew 6:6; Luke 5:15–16; Luke 6:12. Based on these verses, how did Jesus spend his solitude? And how does he tell us to spend ours?

Respond

During this fast, would you be willing to schedule some intentional, lengthier times of solitude? Perhaps a few hours or half a day? Take only your Bible and a journal, turn off your phone, prepare your family for your absence, and devote yourself to listening to the Lord by engaging in Scripture, praying, journaling what you receive from him, and deciding what your next right step is. Write out your plan below.

My Celebration of Solitude

DATE: TIME:

LOCATION: SUPPLIES:

MY PRAYER FOR THIS TIME:

Solitude vs. Loneliness

A 2023 report by the surgeon general of the United States found that our country is fighting a new epidemic: a crisis of loneliness. Chronic loneliness has dangerous impacts on all aspects of health. In fact, loneliness is more dangerous than smoking 15 cigarettes a day.

So why, then, am I telling you to be alone on purpose? The answer lies in understanding that loneliness and solitude are two completely different experiences. For example:

- Solitude is the state of being alone. Loneliness is the emotional anguish that being alone can cause.

- Solitude is a spiritual discipline that's been practiced by believers for centuries. Loneliness is a result of the fall.

- Solitude is peaceful. Loneliness is painful.

Using the Venn diagram below, jot down your thoughts on the differences between ==solitude== and ==loneliness.==

Solitude   Loneliness

What do they have in common? And what sets them apart? Use your answers to guide the decisions you make about practicing solitude.

God Speaks in the Solitude

Use this page to write down any reflections you may have after spending time alone with God.

Without solitude it is virtually impossible to live a spiritual life. We do not take the spiritual life seriously if we do not set aside some time to be with God and listen to him.

Henri Nouwen

Creation and Beauty

Psalm 19:1–6; Ecclesiastes 3:11; Isaiah 40:28

 ## Read

In today's Scripture, we see that the heavens tell the glory of God, and the skies proclaim the work of his hands. Have you thought, really thought, about the fact that everything God has made worships him? The sky, the sun, the moon and stars, the wind and rain, every animal and sea creature, and every tree worships its Maker. The wonder of God's creation and his beauty are all around us. Our God is creative and beautiful in all he does. We see his creativity and beauty everywhere, and it should give us pause to delight in those things as a gift. We should regularly stop and marvel.

During a digital fast, there is more opportunity than ever to not simply look at beauty through photos on our phones, but to get outside and enjoy what no man could create. To imagine the way each of God's creations must be expressing their worship to him. To feel the sun on our faces during the day and try to count the stars at night. There is something grounding and clarifying about remembering the vastness and creativity of God that is experienced in what he has made.

Just as the seasons God has created reveal an aspect of his creativity and character, so too do the seasons of our lives. Ecclesiastes 3:11 tells us that he has made everything beautiful in its time. There is great comfort to be found in knowing God will restore and redeem even the difficult and painful things for our good and his glory. Just as each season of nature peaks and gives way to the next, so we can know the seasons of our lives have come to eventually pass and give way to the next thing God has for us.

🟢 Reflect

What's the most creative or beautiful thing you've seen or experienced recently?

Can you think of a difficult season in your life when you saw God bring beauty out of it?

✒️ Respond

Schedule time to enjoy God's creation in nature by yourself or with others. Spend time in prayer, thanking and praising God.

FIELD
NOTES

Bring this book with you on your outdoor adventures. Observe the world around you and use these pages to slow down, savor the beauty, and record your findings.

The weather today was _____, _____, and _____.

Creatures I saw:

Find a beautiful leaf or flower and paste it here:

Sounds I heard:

The most beautiful thing I observed was:

Being outside today made me curious about:

Draw a picture below of a memorable moment from your outing.

Seasons

God is the author of every season, and each one brings unique gifts. In the grid below, write about the seasons. What do you love about each one? Circle your favorite.

What I love about . . .	
✿ SPRING	☀ SUMMER
🍃 FALL	❄ WINTER

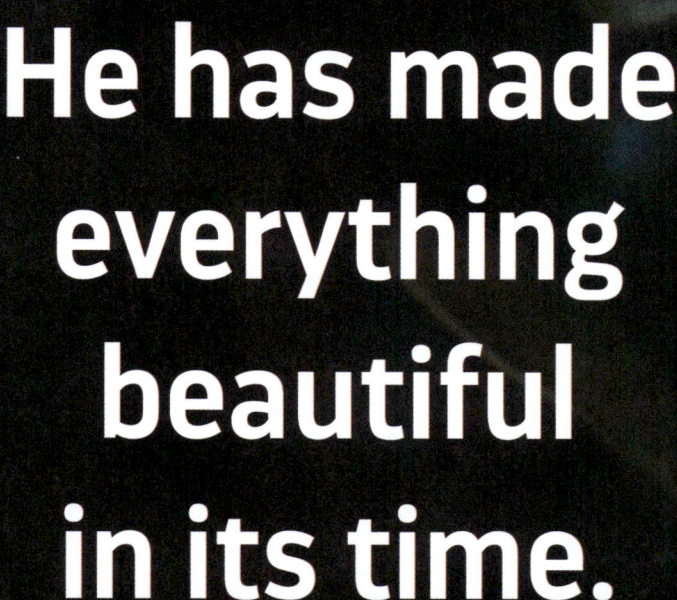

He has made everything beautiful in its time.

Ecclesiastes 3:11 (ESV)

DAY 20	# Free to Play

Job 8:21; Psalm 98:4; Psalm 126:2; Proverbs 15:13;)

 ## Read

They say that laughter is the best medicine, and in many ways, that is true. Laughter often lifts our spirits as few other things can. It helps us cope with life and adds plenty of fun and humorous memories to our relationships. Like God has designed laughter and even given us all a unique laugh, he has also designed us with a specific tendency toward play.

Play reminds us that life is not just work, work, work. God wants us to have times we can just enjoy the life that he's given us with nothing else required. Just as we have been given a unique way to express ourselves in laughter, we each have a style of play that brings us the most joy. Do you know yours? When do you feel most free and unburdened by stress? You may be able to determine your style of play by noticing when you find yourself laughing the most. Do you enjoy physical activity in sports? Or perhaps it's playing card games with friends or working at a hobby or building things with your hands. Maybe you enjoy playing with your kids or cooking with your family. You have a style of play, and you were made for joy and laughter.

When we become adults, we often follow an unwritten rule that says we must be serious and mature, so we craft a life in which play is rare or nonexistent. We may characterize others who prioritize play as immature. In an age where our engagement with devices has the power to sedate us if we're not careful, it seems more important than ever to ensure we're living out all God made us to be. The God who created our laughter experiences joy when he hears us use it. He made it be enjoyed!

Reflect

What keeps you from enjoying more play in life?

How could you intentionally incorporate more play into your life? Write down three ideas.

Respond

Set aside time to laugh and experience play with others.

Check the box next to the activities that sound fun:

☐ Text a dad joke to a friend

☐ Go to a comedy show

☐ Shoot some hoops

☐ Have a dance party in the kitchen

☐ Play with your pet

☐ Play charades

☐ Create a scavenger hunt for your kids

☐ Play a board game

☐ Play a (good-natured) prank

☐ Make a craft

☐ Challenge someone to an arm-wrestling match

☐ Surprise a friend with their favorite treat

☐ Have a silly photoshoot with friends or family

☐ Make a funny home movie

What was your first email address (or AIM username)?

Would you rather have fists the size of nostrils or nostrils the size of fists?

What's a memory that always makes you laugh?

Laughter is contagious.

At your next meal with friends and family, use these conversation questions to get the good times rolling.

Tell a story about something that was embarrassing at the time but now just seems funny.

Who at the table has the most memorable laugh? Prove it.

DAY 21	# Never-Failing Faithfulness
	Psalm 36:5–9; Lamentations 3:22–23; Hebrews 13:8

 ## Read

Of the multiple facets of God's character, his faithfulness is one we can find extreme comfort in. It's impossible for us, as flawed humans, to be fully faithful all the time, even with the best of intentions. We will eventually fail those we love simply because of our own frailty. But God, as a faithful promise keeper, can be counted on never to falter or fail in what he's promised. God can't be contrary to his character, and he can't act in a way that betrays his faithfulness. He does not change like shifting shadows, and this truth gives us reason to put all our confidence in him to come through.

It's because of this truth that you can know God's faithfulness to you never changes. Seasons of weather and seasons of life come and go, but his commitment to you, his promises, and his glory are fixed and immovable. That means you can depend on him to be there when you feel frayed or when a relationship is fracturing. He is with you when others fail you, and though others will let you down, he never will. Even if your faithfulness slips, his won't. In all times and seasons, his faithfulness is as sure as the sunrise and sunset.

As you consider the faithfulness of God during this fast, ask him to bring to your remembrance all the ways he's been faithful. How does knowing God will be faithful embolden you and give you hope in his promises? Is there anything you're waiting on God for? What does his Word say about his faithfulness? Are there specific prayers you could be praying as you wait for him to move? Scripture says the faithfulness of God reaches to the clouds. Let this encourage you—that God's faithfulness to you extends higher than you could ever reach.

Reflect

When was the last time you witnessed God's faithfulness to you?

When was the last time you witnessed God's faithfulness to someone else?

What did you learn about God from those experiences?

Story Time

With your family or friends (or both), share stories of God's past faithfulness.

Follow the instructions on the next page.

1. Find a jar and a pair of scissors.

2. Thinking back on your life, recall stories of times when God has shown his faithfulness to you.

3. Write down a word or phrase that reminds you of each story on the strips to the right.

4. Cut them out and place them in the jar. Invite your loved ones to do the same.

5. Set aside some time to pull out the papers and share stories of God's faithfulness. You could make this a regular occurrence, like over dinner each night.

*The steadfast love of
the Lord never ceases;*

*his mercies never come
to an end;*

*they are new every morning;
great is your faithfulness.*

Lamentations 3:22–23 (ESV)

True or False

I believe that God always keeps his promises.	☐ True	☐ False

What does your answer reveal about your relationship with God?

Determine

Weekly Conversation 4

Establishing Daily Rhythms
by Rebekah Lyons

Rebekah Lyons, author and cofounder of THINQ, explains how life has gotten more chaotic while we've gotten lonelier since the dawn of the Industrial Revolution and the Digital Age. She encourages us to establish life rhythms that help us exchange screens and smartphones for vulnerability and connection. She outlines four life-giving rhythms for emotional, spiritual, and relational health—Rest, Restore, Connect, Create—to best draw and sustain boundaries and make room for a flourishing life.

Watch Rebekah's talk and create conversations around the following:

1. Prior to the digital fast, how had your smartphone and other digital devices affected your rest and restoration? Your connection and your creativity?

2. How have your daily rhythms changed throughout the process of the digital fast?

3. As the twenty-eight-day digital fast ends, what steps could you take to create a sustainable boundary around your devices and each of these daily rhythms: Rest, Restore, Connect, Create?

DAY 22	# Make Up Your Mind
	Romans 12:1–2, 1 Peter 5:7–9

 ## Read

Our Scripture from 1 Peter today starts with a familiar refrain we've heard many times: Cast all your anxiety on him. The rest of this Scripture reminds us that we have an enemy, and he's prowling around, searching for weaknesses he can exploit.

I think today, in much of modern Christianity, we fail to remember that we have a real enemy with real forces and real strategies to oppose and attack God's people. It's important to remember that how we relate to technology and devices can also be discussed in the context of spiritual warfare. Like John 10:10, today's 1 Peter passage is another place where we see the playbook of the enemy. Three times in this tiny letter, Peter said to be alert and of sober mind. Alert means fully awake, paying attention and watching. But watching for what? The enemy, the devil looking for someone to devour. Your enemy has a plan to exploit your unique weaknesses, vulnerabilities, and blind spots. The enemy wants to take you out. But instead of being alert and on guard, instead of engaging in spiritual warfare, we now have millions of God's people whose minds are distracted. Their attention has been ambushed by the powerful and alluring devices we carry around in our pockets.

We're on the home stretch and heading into the last seven days of our twenty-eight days together. By now, you've no doubt made note of some of the changes you've experienced and may even have an idea of what you want to take forward with you once the fast is concluded. Now is the time to resolve to be relentlessly intentional about how you will use digital devices going forward. Our time is too precious to spend any of it letting devices happen to us rather than determining how we'll use them.

 ## Reflect

You have detached yourself from the distraction of your device. Now it's time to be intentionally alert and sober-minded as we come out of this fast.

What habits from this twenty-eight-day journey do you want to carry forward?

Look up this verse and fill in the blanks:

"Do not be _____ to this world, but be _____ by the renewal of your _____."

Romans 12:2 (ESV)

On the Lookout

Some synonyms for "alert" are vigilant, attentive, watchful, on guard, wide awake, and observant.

Practice the skill of being alert:

- Plan an outing to your favorite outdoor spot, a museum, a coffee shop, or a downtown area good for people-watching.

- Bring nothing but this book and a pen or pencil.

- As you settle into your environment, pay attention to what's happening around you. What do your senses pick up?

- Spend at least ten minutes practicing being alert and write your observations below:

My Observations

How does it feel to be fully awake to the world around you?

Respond

We all prioritize certain things. We all won't do certain things. We all have some kind of bedtime routine. We all eat a certain way. We prioritize certain spiritual practices. As you've cleared your mind these past few weeks, what priorities have become clear to you? Make a list of your top ten below, in no particular order:

My Top 10 Priorities

01 _____

02 _____

03 _____

04 _____

05 _____

06 _____

07 _____

08 _____

09 _____

10 _____

Now, narrow that list down to the **top five**:

01 _____   02 _____

03 _____   04 _____

05 _____

Finally, define your **top three priorities**:

01 _____   02 _____

03 _____

What changes do you need to make to your digital consumption to protect those priorities?

Protect Your Priorities

It's impossible to protect your priorities without firm boundaries, especially when it comes to technology.

Aro is a screen time solution for families. It helps you spend less time on your phones and reclaim that time for the things that matter. Rather than block or limit screen time, Aro develops the habit of physically putting your phone down when you want to focus, engage, connect, or simply be present.

For parents, Aro enables you to model the right relationship and behaviors with your own device, which sets up your kids for success when they eventually have a device of their own.

As part of your participation in the digital fast, you have access to Aro for free throughout your journey and for your thirty days of reentry. If you have not done so already, just scan the custom *Digital Fast* QR code below to redeem your sixty-day free Aro journey or email support@goaro.com for help.

DAY 23	# Made for Flourishing
	Matthew 5:13–16; Colossians 3:23–24; James 2:14–26

 ## Read

A lush garden is something to behold. When its flowers are in full bloom, or the fruits and vegetables are plump and ripe, it teems with life and vitality. We were made to be like that garden because God made us to flourish. Adam and Eve were put in a garden, and God called them to tend it. They were also called to be fruitful and multiply. Like them, we are called to tend the garden of our lives with good works that bear fruit that multiplies. Just like a garden needs regular attention and work, we need to pay regular attention to the opportunities before us to do something to bring flourishing into our lives and the lives of others.

What has God gifted and called you to do? Do you lead people or teams? Do you work with your hands? Are you bringing something good into the lives of others? Do you know how you can carry out good works in what God has made you for? Opportunities to do good in the lives of others aren't often just sitting in front of us in an obvious way. Part of being awake and alert to the world around us is remembering that we're ambassadors of God's goodness on earth and looking for ways to dispense it.

Even the healthiest garden, left unattended, will sprout and spread weeds that choke out the flourishing life. When we consider our own lives, weeds can certainly look like sin that needs to be dealt with before the Lord, but they can also be things like distraction. When we're distracted and not awake to the needs and opportunities around us, that can be a type of weed that chokes out invitations to spread God's goodness. You have good works designed especially for you and your specific gifts, which are your contribution to God's kingdom. As we finish this fast, consider how you can tend to the weeds in your garden to provide opportunities for flourishing in your God-given calling.

✒ Respond

In what ways has your relationship with digital technology and your devices kept you from tending the garden of your life?

How could a changed relationship with them produce more fruit and good works in your life?

Bloom Where You're Planted

Go on a walk in your neighborhood. Notice the flowers that grow close by. Pick one (get permission if it's from a neighbor's yard!) and tape it to this page.

If it's not the season for flowers or you live in a concrete jungle, sketch your favorite flower in the space above. What do you love about it?

Pulling Up the Weeds

In today's reading, you learned that **distraction is a major weed** that chokes out our ability to flourish and help those around us flourish. What other weeds of sin are keeping you from growth? Name them below.

Ex: Distraction

Reflect

Without expectation of getting anything in return, do something for someone else today. Show kindness. Be generous. Whatever it is, do something that gives someone else a picture of the flourishing life God wants for us. After your good deed, reflect on your experience below.

Who did you choose to bless?

What did you do?

What happened?

Life in the Spirit
Galatians 5

 Read

What does a fruitful, flourishing life look like? Paul showed us in his letter to the Galatians as he contrasted two ways of living—life in the flesh and life in the Spirit. Life in the flesh isn't pretty. But contrast that life with life in the Spirit: "But the fruit of the Spirit is love, joy, peace, forbearance, kindness, goodness, faithfulness, gentleness and self-control. Against such things there is no law" (vv. 22–23 NIV).

What is love? We love everything from spaghetti to TV shows, but what does real love look like? First Corinthians 13 has a few things to say. This is the primary way Jesus said others would know we're his, by our love. Joy is a state of being that transcends circumstances or feelings. How does deep, abiding joy manifest itself, and how do we hold onto it no matter what we're facing? The joy of the Lord can really be our strength. In a culture that's flailing and splitting at the seams, we are in desperate need of people of peace. Far from being doormats or acquiescing to ideas we don't believe in or agree with, peace is a state of being, a settled confidence. It's a willingness to be peaceful over being right, believing that God is the true upholder of our cause.

Instant gratification is now everywhere. We are losing the art of patience, but what does patience have to teach us? When God asks us to wait, we are sitting in fertile soil to increase our faith and dependence. This world needs people who are kind. Too often, we feign kindness externally while being the furthest from kind internally. Social media feeds our unkindness as we sit in positions of judgment and eavesdrop on one another. May we be people who are actually kind. Goodness is probably the least understood or talked about fruit of the Spirit. When someone is infused with goodness, they practice goodness thoroughly. What would true goodness look like in each of our lives?

Our God has provided the ultimate example of faithfulness. How can our lives reflect the faithfulness of God in the things we do and say, the relationships around us, and our devotion to Him? "Let your gentleness be evident to all. The Lord is near" (Philippians 4:5 NIV). What does this have to do with our gentleness? Letting the Holy Spirit work gentleness in us has implications beyond us and extends to others. We are only able to practice self-control through the power of the Holy

Spirit. This same power that raised Christ from the dead is within us, and when harnessed, it helps us be conscious of controlling not only our actions but our words and thoughts.

The fruit of the Spirit is what transforms our life. Let us use our thoughts, words, and actions to produce more of the fruit of the Spirit in the garden of our lives and relationships.

Reflect

Look at the fruit of the Spirit below. Which of these would you like to see more of in your life? Circle two or three that stand out.

LOVE	FORBEARANCE	FAITHFULNESS
JOY	KINDNESS	GENTLENESS
PEACE	GOODNESS	SELF-CONTROL

How would you be different if there were more fruit in your life and relationships?

✒ Respond

With your family and friends, focus on one aspect of the fruit of the Spirit and how you might produce more of that with thoughts, words, and actions. You can focus on other aspects in subsequent weeks if you like.

The fruit I am choosing is _____.

List ways this fruit could manifest in your thoughts, words, and actions:		
THOUGHTS	WORDS	ACTIONS

The Smartphone Parenting Model

We are called to imitate our heavenly Father as "dearly beloved children" (Ephesians 5:1) by producing fruit of the Spirit. Sadly, however, many of us are modeling a different set of behaviors for those around us. And who sees and imitates our behavior most often? Our children. Over the last seventeen years, we've adopted the 3Ms of the smartphone parenting model:

- We as parents **Model** a less-than-ideal relationship with our phones (we phone snub our kids, we check texts at the dinner table, etc.).

- At some point, we give our kids a phone and they **Mimic** what we have modeled to them (they phone snub *us*, they check messages at the dinner table, etc.).

- At this point, we do something crazy. We get **Mad** at our kids for mimicking what we have modeled to them.

This is no judgment, by the way. We are all learning as we go and we are doing our best. Aro proposes good news: We can flip the script on this narrative.

What if we **Model** a great relationship with our phones, like using Aro at dinner or putting down our screens when we are speaking with our kids? Then our kids are more likely **Mimic** that great relationship and we can **Make Memories** or **Magical Moments** or any other cool M you can think of!

| DAY 25 | # Staying Connected to the Vine
John 15:1–8 |

 ## Read

There are people in our lives we love to linger with. You probably have that friend or family member with whom you never want the conversation to end. Your time with them could go late into the night or past closing time at the coffee shop. Being with these people adds joy, light, laughter, and wisdom to life. You simply enjoy being with them because there's no agenda other than to be together. Have you ever considered that Jesus wants a similar relationship with you? In John 15, he showed us that's precisely what he wants. He wants us to linger with him. The way Jesus put it is that he wants us to "abide" with him. To spend time with him. To stay with him. To remain with him.

Along with the fruit of the Spirit, abiding in Jesus is another way to bear fruit in our lives. When we stay connected to him, we stay connected to the life source that makes growth, fruit, and flourishing possible. As we seek to abide in him during this fast, it's important for us to remember just who he is to us. He is our good shepherd, our refuge, our strong tower, and our intercessor.

Hudson Taylor once said, "The branch of the vine does not worry, and toil, and rush here to seek for sunshine, and there to find rain. No, it rests in union and communion with the vine; and at the right time, and in the right way, is the right fruit found on it. Let us so abide in the Lord Jesus." Union and communion. No worry, toil, or rush. When we simply remain with Jesus and let his life be our life, we find him gently leading and guiding us, providing rest, holding us close, and strengthening us. As we move toward the end of this fast, consider how you will prioritize lingering with Jesus.

 ## Reflect

What about your life now makes it difficult for you to linger with Jesus?

What changes could you make to prioritize the relationship he wants with you?

Linger (verb):
To stay in a place longer than
necessary because of a reluctance
to leave

Who helps you linger?

In the box below, write the name of someone you simply enjoy being with—someone you can talk to for hours, long past the closing time at a coffee shop:

Now, get out your phone and send them a text telling them how much you appreciate them. Better yet, call them and set up a time to get together.

Did You Know?

According to research, 91% of us have our phones with us 24 hours a day.[1]

In other words, you spend more time with your phone than anything (or anyone) else. As a result, we are battling the allure of our phones on a near-constant basis. We are more connected to the glow of our screens than the vine of Christ.

1. Morgan Stanley Research, 2012.

 ## Respond

Let your family and close relationships in on your desire to be intentional about lingering with Jesus and ask for their help in prioritizing it.

When is the next time you will spend time—and linger—with Jesus?

DATE: _____   TIME: _____

DAY 26 — Remaining in His Love

John 15:9–17

Read

In John 15, Jesus told his disciples that the love the Father has for him is the same love he had for them. This is the kind of love that Jesus wants us to remain in as his followers. How do we do that? Jesus tells us—by keeping his commands. When we follow the way of Jesus and his teaching, we experience more of the abundant and flourishing life he promised to give us. It isn't complicated. We also experience the Father's love for us in greater and greater degrees.

This is a beautiful cycle of love. The Father loves the Son, and the Son loves the Father. The Son gives the love of the Father to his followers. And we, his followers—now God's children—receive that love and give it right back to him. This cycle of remaining in his love is another example of what it means to abide, but our hearts must be available and open to receive the Father's love if we hope to give it to others.

Proverbs 4:23 reminds us to guard our hearts with all diligence because everything we do flows from it. Abiding in Christ means recognizing the necessity of a heart that is led rather than a heart that is leading. When we are meditating on the truth of Jesus, our feelings and heart attitudes will be engaged in emotions that glorify Him and enable growth in our lives. These are the springs of life. When these springs are flowing unhindered in our lives, we not only receive the love of Jesus, but it flows from us and to others.

Respond

Devote an evening to simply remaining in Jesus's love by taking some time to just abide. You can choose however you want to do that. It can be creative or simple. It can be worshipping through prayer or song. It can be going to a park or field in the middle of nowhere. Whatever it is, your main agenda is remaining in Jesus's love with no distractions, especially from digital technology. Write your plan below.

🟢 Reflect

How have you experienced Jesus's love for you recently?

What Abiding Looks Like

Draw a picture of what comes to mind when you hear the word "abide."

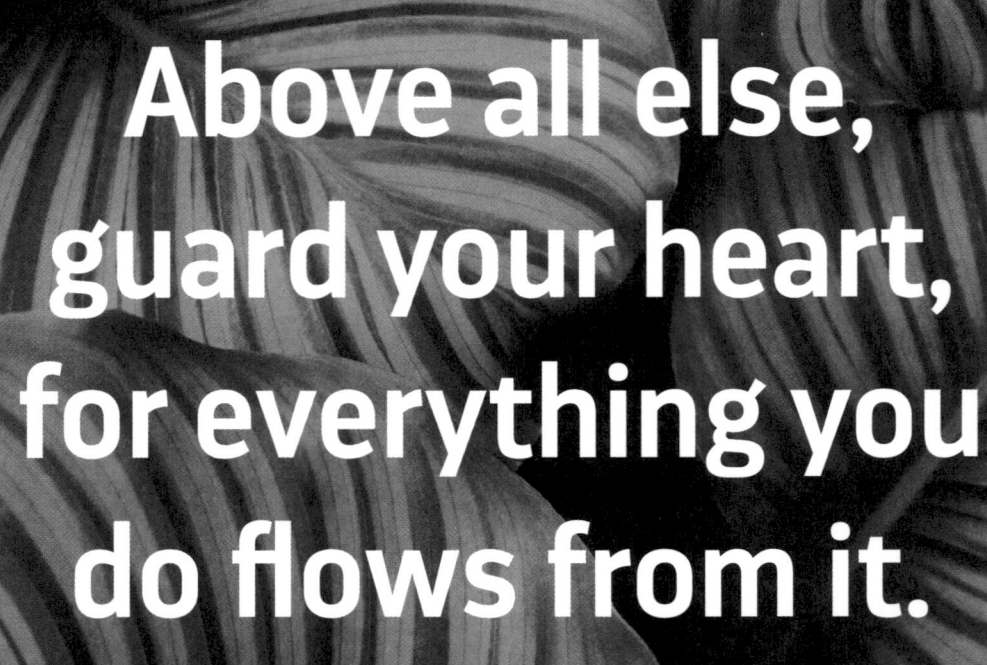

Above all else, guard your heart, for everything you do flows from it.

Proverbs 4:23 (NIV)

What's the state of your heart?
What is flowing out of you these days?
Write your thoughts inside the heart below.

Break the Screen Time Cycle

In today's reading, we learned about the cycle of love that exists between the Father, the Son, and us as God's children.

Unfortunately, many of us find ourselves stuck in another cycle that Aro calls the "PID Loop." PID stands for Proximity, Interaction, and Dependence.

Aro proposes we break the cycle by cutting off our Proximity to our phones for periods of time per day. By separating ourselves, we Interact less with our phones and become less Dependent on them. And if we are less Dependent on them, we won't feel the need to always be in Proximity to them, putting a halt to the PID Loop.

Brainstorm a few ideas for cutting off proximity to your phone:

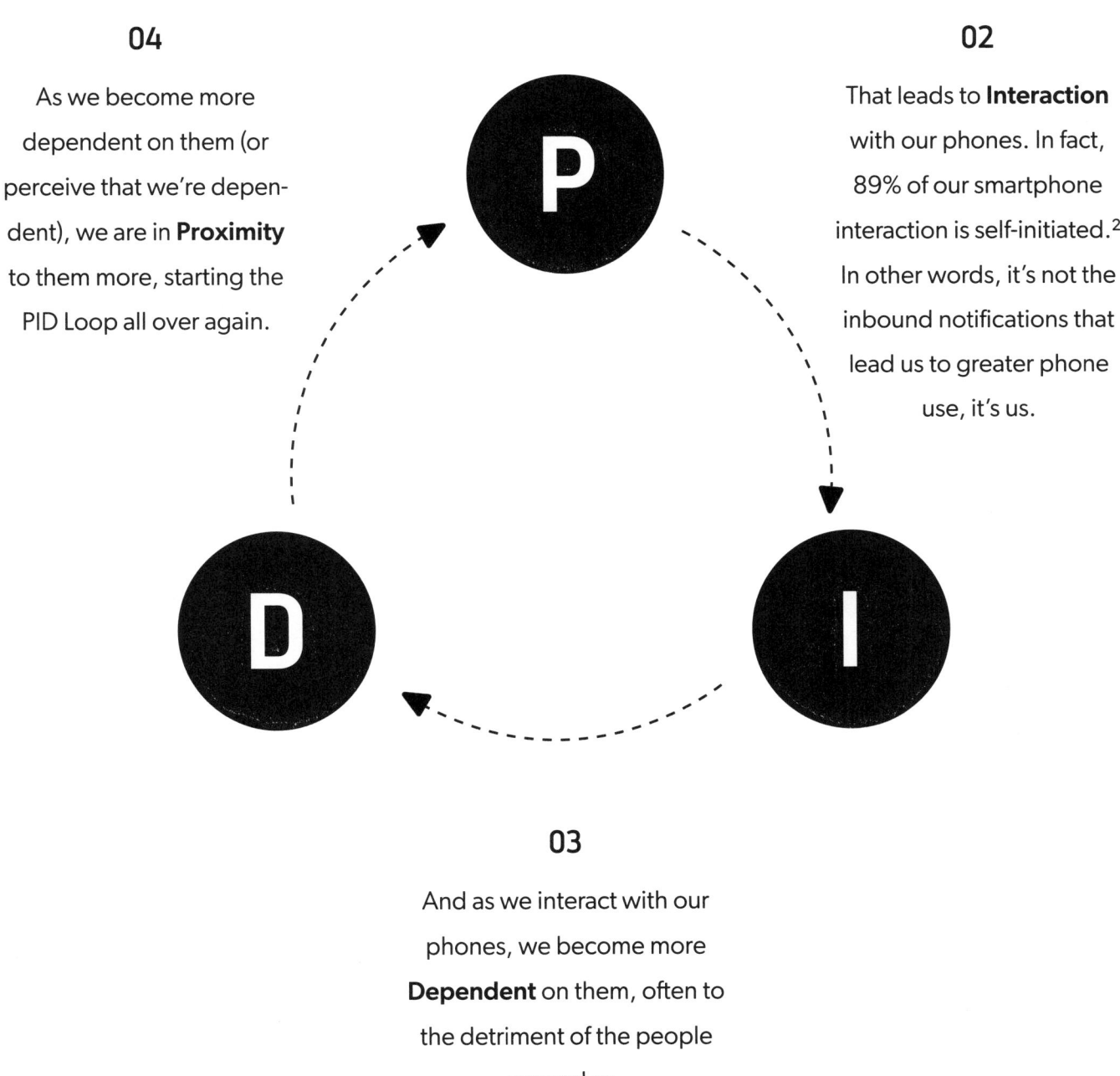

01

The Loop begins with our **Proximity** to our phones—they are with us 24 hours per day.

04

As we become more dependent on them (or perceive that we're dependent), we are in **Proximity** to them more, starting the PID Loop all over again.

02

That leads to **Interaction** with our phones. In fact, 89% of our smartphone interaction is self-initiated.[2] In other words, it's not the inbound notifications that lead us to greater phone use, it's us.

03

And as we interact with our phones, we become more **Dependent** on them, often to the detriment of the people around us.

2. "Smartphone use and smartphone addiction: A Q&A with Maxi Heitmayer," The London School of Economics and Personal Finance, accessed September 28, 2024, https://www.lse.ac.uk/Research/researcher-profiles/Maxi-Heitmayer.

| DAY 27 | What Does Jesus Ask of Us? |

 ## Read

In *Emotionally Healthy Spirituality*[3], Peter Scazzero writes about the concept of a Rule of Life:

Very few people have a conscious plan for developing their spiritual lives. Most Christians are not intentional, but rather functional, like cars on autopilot. Our crammed schedules, endless to-do lists, demanding jobs and families, constant noise, information bombardment, and anxieties keep us speeding up, not slowing down. We have routines to manage other parts of our lives. For example, each morning we may get up, feed the cat, then make coffee, exercise, get dressed for work, and eat breakfast.

The reality, however, is that every person has an unconscious Rule for developing his or her spiritual life. We each have our values and ways of doing things. This may include, for example, attending a church on Sundays, participating in a small group, serving in a ministry, and/or ten minutes for prayer and Bible reading before going to bed.

However, our present spiritual practices are not enough to keep us afloat in the ocean of the beast, the Babylon of our twenty-first century world. Fighting against such a strong current, without the anchor of a Rule of Life, is almost impossible. Eventually we find ourselves unfocused, distracted, and adrift spiritually.

Nurturing a growing spirituality with depth in our present-day culture will require a thoughtful, conscious, intentional plan for our spiritual lives.

The great, buried gift in a Rule of Life is its goal of regulating our entire lives in such a way that we truly prefer the love of Christ above all things.

God has made each of us unique and different. Our goal is the same: union with God in Christ, transformation into his image, and the freeing of our hearts from anything that stands in the way of Christ living in and through us. How we get there will vary, depending on our personality, gift mix, temperament, geographic location, and particular calling from God. In addition, God will have different practices and emphases at different seasons and phases of our lives.

3. Peter Scazzero, Emotionally Healthy Spiritually: It's Impossible to Be Spiritually Mature While Remaining Emotionally Immature (Zondervan, 2017), 190–193.

What if you were to apply the concept of a Rule of Life to create a Digital Rule of Life to regulate your relationship with digital technology and your devices so that you prefer Jesus and his love above all else? Would that make a significant difference in how you live? I'm confident it would, so I'm encouraging you to create a Digital Rule of Life for you (and your family).

Before doing that, ask yourself, "What does Jesus ask of me and my life as it relates to my relationship with digital technology and my devices?" As you reflect on that question with Jesus, consider how God's Word helps with the answer. Jesus asks for our . . .

- Love (John 13:34–35)
- Obedience (Matthew 7:24–29)
- Humility (Philippians 2:3–11)
- Faithfulness (Hebrews 11:1–40)
- Endurance (Romans 5:3–4; Hebrews 12:1–3)

Reflect

What is Jesus asking of you and your life regarding your relationship with digital technology and your devices?

What's the better life he wants for you?

What changes would be required for you to experience the life he wants for you?

"A Rule of Life is a trellis that helps us abide in Christ and become more fruitful spiritually."

Peter Scazzero

 Respond

Begin creating your Digital Rule of Life. Start by reading Chapter 10 of *The Digital Fast*.

Consider how you want to change your relationship with digital technology and your devices in various life areas. Don't rush through this activity. Devote time and prayer to it because it is the Digital Rule of Life you (and your family) will live by.

My Digital Rule of Life

How do you want to change your relationship with devices in each of the following areas? Begin gathering your thoughts below.

Spiritual	
Relational	
Physical	
Emotional	

Intellectual	
Vocational	
Financial	
Recreational	

<table>
<tr><td>DAY 28</td><td># A New Way of Living
John 17</td></tr>
</table>

 ## Read

One of the most touching episodes in the Bible is Jesus's High Priestly Prayer in the upper room just before his arrest. Jesus lifted his eyes to the Father and prayed to be glorified. He prayed for his disciples in the room with him, and then he prayed for us. If we spend time in this prayer, we will discover even more of what Jesus wants for us and our lives. Jesus knew what was ahead of him. He would be crucified and die, but death wouldn't keep him in the grave. He would rise on the third day and triumph over his—and our—enemies. From there, he would call his disciples to spread the good news about a new way of living.

Verse 17 (ESV) of today's reading says, "Sanctify them in the truth; your word is truth." After Jesus prayed for our protection from the evil one, he prayed for the protection of our sanctification, that it would be covered in truth. Then he provided the source of that truth. God's Word is truth. In a world full of shifting ideologies and subjective opinions, the Scriptures act as both our baseline and our filter for everything else.

Because of our constant exposure to lies, we must remain sanctified in truth. We are accused by the father of lies all day, every day. He uses each area of weakness, sin, insecurity, and pride within us to his advantage. If we're not on our guard and sanctified in truth, we will believe his lies. As we commit ourselves to abiding in Christ, we can be confident the enemy will turn up the volume on those lies as much as he can, especially as we search for a new and healthier way forward with digital technology.

It's not up to us to navigate truth and lies on our own. We have the source of all truth in our grasp. Abiding in Christ means studying him and his truth, and no one else can do it for us. That new way of living is available to us today. Jesus prayed for it for us. As we finalize and implement our Digital Rule of Life, we can know we're being led by a wise God to a new way and that his promise still stands.

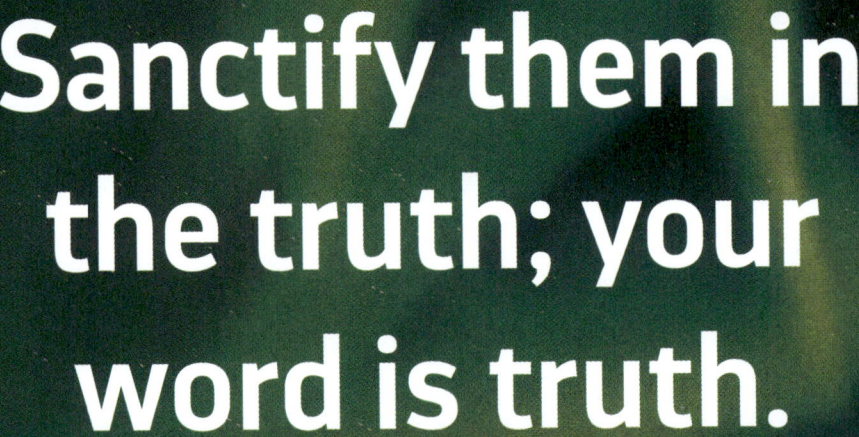

Sanctify them in the truth; your word is truth.

John 17:17 (ESV)

How often do you consume the truth by spending time in God's Word?

What (if anything) would you like to change about that habit?

Reflect

What will be most challenging about implementing your Digital Rule of Life?

How can others help you overcome that challenge?

Respond

Finish your Digital Rule of Life and share it with others. Compare yours and theirs to learn something you might want to integrate into your own Digital Rule of Life. Commit to following up as a community about how things are going (what's been great, what's been difficult) and encourage one another in the new way of living Jesus calls us into.

My Digital Rule of Life

Reentry

How to Think Well (THINQ Framework)
by Gabe Lyons

Gabe Lyons, founder and president of THINQ, challenges us to go beyond social media and Google search to get information and knowledge. He implores us to become people who think well by introducing the five-part THINQ rubric as a transformational framework to understand and navigate the chaos and manipulation of our current culture. He encourages us to become thought leaders—people who can discern the lies of the world, call them out, and inject truth and wisdom in the places and spaces God has us.

Watch Gabe's talk and create conversations around the following:

1. After walking through the phases of the digital fast, how have you found yourself asking better questions about your smartphone and other technological devices?

2. How can you think well and apply the THINQ Framework [T–Theology, H–History, I–Inquiry, N–Nuance, Q–Questions] to your new understanding and prioritization of technology in your life?

3. Beyond the digital fast, how could you continue to create conversations that would lead to wisdom around technology and other pressing issues in culture?

Breaking the Fast

As you prepare for reentry, take a few minutes to reflect on the past twenty-eight days.
Write down your answers to the questions below.

What did you learn about God, yourself, and others?

How have you grown in the past twenty-eight days? Where do you want to continue to grow?

What did you enjoy most about your fast that you want to continue?

What did you start or stop doing that made you feel more alive?

How are you different after going through the digital fast?

In what ways did you engage with others that you want to carry over?

Life on the Other Side

You and your community have gone through twenty-eight days of a digital fast. My hope is that you have experienced more of life as it was meant to be lived. My hope is that you have discovered a lot about God, yourself, and your relationship with digital technology and your devices. My hope is that having done a digital detox, you don't want to do a digital "retox."

On the other side of the twenty-eight-day digital fast, you must determine to live differently. Without an intentional plan, it will be that much easier to go back to the way things were. Why? Because in many ways, the habits you formed with digital technology and your devices made life more comfortable. And we know that our enemy will use comfort to draw us back, because we are creatures of habit who prefer what's easiest.

Living differently will require effort, determination, and total reliance on God and the help of others in your community to choose life and the better way Jesus gives us. Committing to your Digital Rule of Life is key to life on the other side.

Church Camp High

Did you ever attend a church camp growing up? If you did, I'm sure you remember the "spiritual high" you felt. You were on top of the world, close to God, and deeply connected to your brothers and sisters in Christ. These memorable moments are charged with feeling. But after a week or two of being home, you experienced a disappointing reality check: Church camp highs can't sustain us forever. That's why spiritual daily disciplines, like reading the Word, praying, and serving, are critical. Church camp experiences are an important part of our walk with God, but our ongoing spiritual rhythms are what sustain us.

You might feel like the twenty-eight-day digital fast has been a "church camp" experience. You've been intentional about your relationship with God for four weeks straight, and now, you're stepping back into "real life," as we say. If you use this experience as a launching pad into a healthy digital life, I firmly believe you can carry the deep connection you've formed with God into the days ahead.

So, what does a healthy daily digital life looks like?

Over the past several years, I have gotten to know a company called Aro, which helps with daily digital life. I have no affiliation to Aro but have gotten to know their team and solution and believe it is the best tool to help you with reentry. Here's how it works:

Aro believes the primary problem we have with our phones is a relationship issue—our relationships with our phones are getting in the way of our most important relationships. The defining characteristic of our relationship with our phones is our constant proximity to them. In fact, 91% of us have our phones with us 24 hours per day. As a result, we are battling the allure of the phone on a near-constant basis. So it's no wonder we phone snub our families at the dinner table or can't focus during a conversation.

As a guiding principle for your reentry, Aro encourages you to Start-Stop: Start with yourself. It's far too easy to point the finger at those around us when it comes to phone habits—our spouses, our parents, our friends, or society in general. But as you reenter the world, we encourage you to take Aro's advice and Start with yourself.

After starting with yourself, Aro encourages you to Stop at nothing to sustain healthy digital habits. You participated in the digital fast for a reason. Maybe someone forced you into it, but my guess is you felt some need to do it for yourself. As a society, we recognize how high the stakes are. Our relationships depend on it. Our kids' futures depend on it. Aro says that every good thing we want in life depends on it. All the great relationships we have will be limited by our relationship with our phone.

Aro is the best tool to help you "stop at nothing" and sustain your digital wellness throughout the year. Aro is a screen time solution for families. It helps you spend less time on your phones and reclaim that time for the things that matter. Rather than block or limit screen time, Aro develops the habit of physically putting your phone down when you want to focus, engage, connect, or simply be present.

For parents, Aro enables you to model the right relationship and behaviors with your own device, which sets up your kids for success when they eventually have a device of their own.

As part of your participation in the digital fast, you have access to Aro for free throughout your journey and for your thirty days of reentry. If you have not done so already, just scan the custom *Digital Fast* QR code below to redeem your sixty-day free Aro journey or email support@goaro.com for help.

Reentry Checklist

☐ Live out and refine your Digital Rule of Life.

☐ Share your Digital Rule of Life with those close to you. Change comes collectively.

☐ Read the Conclusion of *The Digital Fast.*

☐ Try the Aro app for free to cement your new digital habits.

☐ Have grace for yourself (and others) as you begin your new digital life.

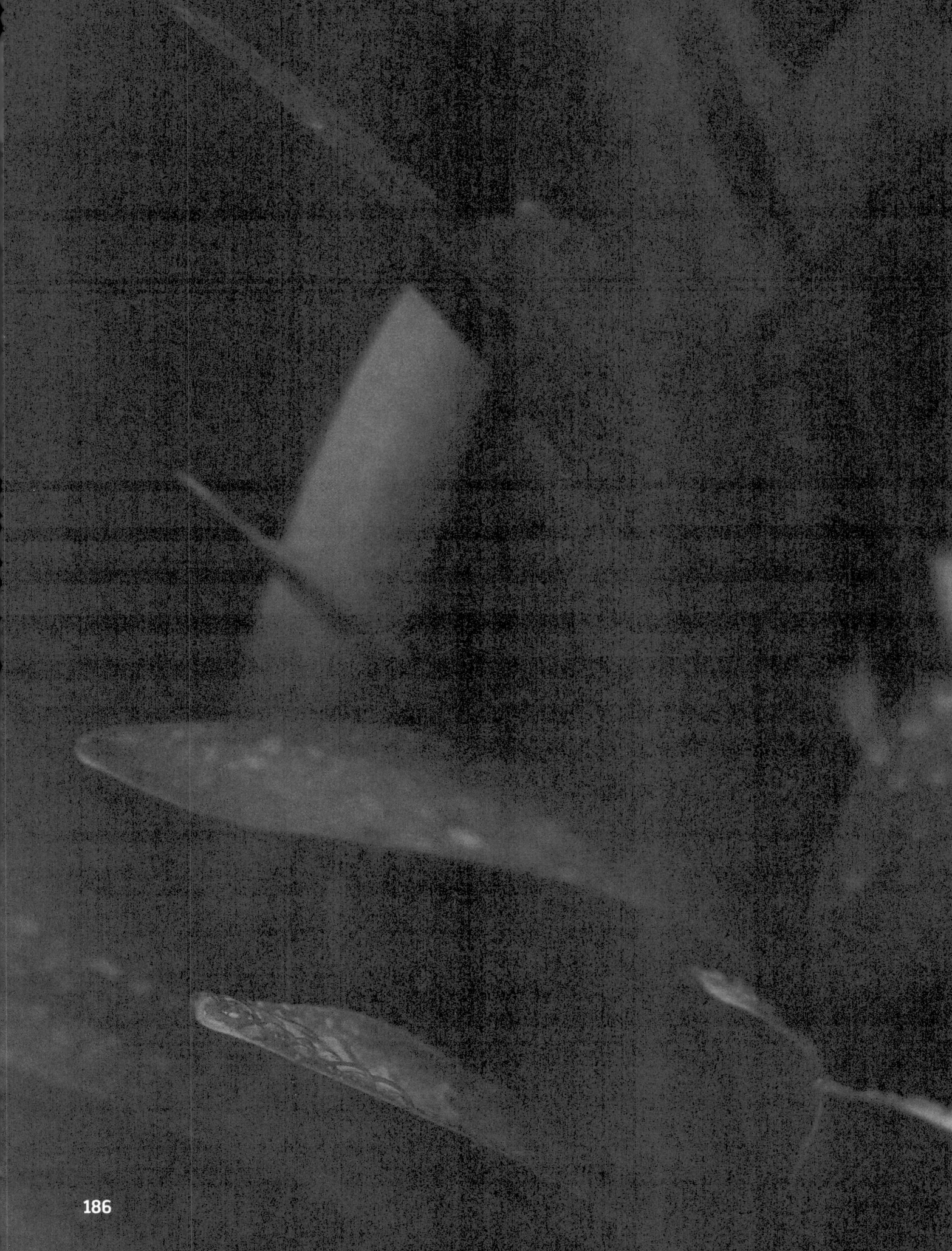

Abundant Life

John 10:10 (ESV) has been a familiar verse throughout our time together. In it, Jesus tells us, "The thief comes only to steal and kill and destroy. I came that they may have life and have it abundantly."

My prayer for you on the other side of this fast is that you continually choose abundant life in Christ. May you put down your screens and be captivated by the people and the beauty around you. May you refuse to engage in mindless distraction. May you set an example for your family, your friends, and the body of Christ—because any lasting change we wish to make must be collective.

Welcome back to the world of tech, with a heart full of joy and a phone full of purpose.

Grace and peace.

Darren Whitehead

Acknowledgments

Like all things that really matter, this book project had a team of people, often unseen, who have worked tirelessly to make this come to life. I am profoundly grateful for you all.

My wife, Brandy, thanks for believing in this idea and helping to create space to share it beyond our church. My daughters, Sydney, Scarlett and Violet, thanks for all your thoughts and feedback and for being my primary focus group.

Angie LoSchiavo, my amazing assistant. You and the Big Eagle are rams! Brandy and I thank God for you daily! Thanks for all the things I know and for all the things I don't even know, you did!

Heath Wilson, Joey Odom & the whole ARO team, what can I say? You guys have jumped into this project with both feet. I can't thank you enough!

Gabe & Rebekah Lyons, Jackie Quinn & the whole THINQ Media team. Thanks for being so supportive & getting behind this collective action problem.

Rachel Miller, you have been a force behind this workbook coming to life. Thanks for pouring your heart into it. Shannon Scott, thanks for lending your brilliant creativity, research, insight and writing skills to this idea. Both when we did this as a church family and also this book project.

Josh Webb & Christine Birch, your graphic design work is simply stunning! I am so thankful for you both pouring your creativity into this project!

Jason and Steph Child, thanks for always showing such support. We are so thankful for you. Scott Harrison, for that lunch at BrickTops which became the seed of this project.

The Church of the City family, thanks for having such an entrepreneurial spirit and the courage to push back against our culture and embrace a churchwide digital fast.

About The Author

Darren Whitehead

Originally from Australia, Darren has lived in the United States for over 25 years. In 2013, he founded Church of the City, now with several locations across Nashville. He earned his Masters in Ministry from Wesley Seminary and his Doctorate from Capital Seminary and Graduate School, with his dissertation focus on Millennials and the future of the Western church. Darren's previous books include, Rumors of God (co-authored with Jon Tyson) and Holy Roar (co-authored with Chris Tomlin).

Darren lives with his wife, Brandy, and their three daughters in Franklin, Tennessee.
For more resources on *The Digital Fast,* go to: thedigitalfast.com

For more resources visit:

thedigitalfast.com

The Digital Fast

This book is a twenty-eight-day guided journey to turn down digital distraction and turn up spiritual devotion. This includes "making your smartphone dumb" by removing apps that provide "distraction" (social media, games, news, email etc.) and then only using your smartphone for "utility" functions (phone, text, calendar, camera etc.) By turning down the digital noise, you will experience the time, space and mental clarity to reconnect with those around you and hear the voice of God.